William Andrews

Bygone England

Social Studies in its Historic Byways and Highways

William Andrews

Bygone England
Social Studies in its Historic Byways and Highways

ISBN/EAN: 9783744763929

Printed in Europe, USA, Canada, Australia, Japan

Cover: Foto ©Suzi / pixelio.de

More available books at **www.hansebooks.com**

Bygone England:

Social Studies in its Historic Byways and Highways.

BY

WILLIAM ANDREWS, F.R.H.S.,

AUTHOR OF

"OLD CHURCH LORE," "CURIOSITIES OF THE CHURCH,"
"OLD-TIME PUNISHMENTS," ETC., ETC.

LONDON :

HUTCHINSON & CO.

1892.

TO

GEORGE AUGUSTUS SALA

THIS VOLUME IS DEDICATED

AS A TOKEN OF

ESTEEM AND ADMIRATION

Preface.

AN attempt is made in this volume to illustrate some phases of the social life of England in the olden time. The book represents the study of many years, made in out-of-the-way places and amongst books and manuscripts which do not usually come under the notice of the general reader. I am not indifferent as to its reception from the public and the press, and I trust that it may meet with the same friendly welcome that has been accorded to my previous works.

All the articles in this volume have been written with a view of publication in book form, although a few have previously appeared in the pages of *Chambers's Journal*, *Home Chimes*, the *British Workwoman*, and other periodicals.

WILLIAM ANDREWS.

HULL LITERARY CLUB.
August 11th, 1892.

Contents.

BYGONE ENGLAND.

Under Watch and Ward.

IN the days of long ago, towns were surrounded by walls where men known as warders paced by day and night, and kept a sharp outlook to announce the approach of friend or foe. References in prose and poetry to the practice frequently occur in our literature. A familiar instance is that contained in Scott's "Marmion." He thus describes the watch in the evening:

> " The warriors on the turrets high,
>   Moving athwart the evening sky,
>   Seemed forms of giant height :
>   Their armour, as it caught the rays,
>   Flash'd back again the western blaze,
>   In lines of dazzling light.

> " Saint George's banner, broad and gay,
>   Now faded, as the fading ray
>   Less bright, and less, was flung ;
>   The evening gale had scarce the power
>   To waive it on the Donjon Tower,
>   So heavily it hung.

"The scouts had parted on their search,
    The castle gates were barred ;
Above the gloomy portal arch,
Timing his footsteps to a march,
    The warder kept his guard ;
Low humming, as he paced along,
Some ancient Border gathering song."

After the age had passed away when towns had to be guarded against the attacks of foreign and other foes, protection from one another was afforded to the inhabitants by watchmen.

WARDER'S TOWER, CASTLE, ASHBY-DE-LA-ZOUCH.

Henry III. had serious disputes with the citizens of London, and it was in his troublesome times that we find the first notice of a nightly watch in London. In the year 1253, the King ordered a strong guard of horsemen, supported by infantry, to patrol the streets nightly. This guard gave rise to a gang of thieves, who, under the pretence of searching for aliens, broke into

houses and carried away goods. To stop
robbery, a more efficient watch had to be
instituted. The mounted watch was discontinued,
and in its place a permanent watch was established.
London and other large cities were divided into
wards; over each an alderman was appointed,
who usually acted as magistrate, and in other
ways attended to the interests of the ward.
Considerable power was placed in the hands
of the members of the watch. Improper
characters and suspected persons might be taken
into custody by them, and detained for trial on
the following day. In these earlier times lusty
young men, well armed and able to deal with any
ruffians they met on their rounds, formed the
watch. The class of men degenerated, and in
later times poor worn-out fellows filled the position
of night watchmen.

The famous Statute of Winchester, passed in
1285, directs that two high constables be chosen
for every hundred, and that they report to the
King's justice and arrest "all suspicious night-
walkers." This statute, altered and amended
from time to time, was in force during more than
five centuries.

The London watch in Tudor times was a large

and able body of men.   In 1509, Henry VIII. made
his entry in state into the city of London, and was
received with great pomp and pageantry, the chief
attraction being the parading of the watch before
his Majesty.   It is asserted that the procession so
greatly pleased the King, that he shortly afterwards returned with his Queen and the principal
nobility to witness it.   It was afterwards continued
for many years every Midsummer night.   From
old-time accounts of this annual gathering we get a
good idea of its splendour.

A programme of the procession is as
follows :—" The march was begun by the
City music ; followed by the Lord Mayor's
officers in parti-coloured liveries ; the sword-
bearer on horseback, in beautiful armour,
preceded the Lord Mayor, mounted on a stately
horse, richly trapped, attended by a giant and
two pages on horseback, three pageants, morris-
dancers, and footmen ; next came the sheriffs
preceded by their officers, and attended by their
giants, pages, pageants, and morris-dancers ;
then marched a great body of demi-lances,
in bright armour, on stately horses ; next
followed a body of carabineers, in white fustian
coats, with a symbol of the City arms on their

backs and breasts : then marched a division
of archers, with their bows bent, and shafts of
arrows by their sides ; next followed a party of

THE WATCH, WITH CRESSETS AND BEACONS, GROUPED FROM HOLLAR.

pikemen in their corselets and helmets ; after
whom marched a column of halberdiers in their
corselets and helmets, and the march was closed

by a great party of billmen, with helmets and aprons of mail, and the whole body consisting of about two thousand men, had between every division a certain number of musicians, who were answered in their proper places by the like number of drums, with standards and ensigns, as veteran troops."

A striking feature of the procession was the illumination made by the burning of 940 cressets. The cost of these was a heavy sum of money. The City paid for 200, the Companies of London paid for 500, and the City constables paid for the remaining 240. Two men had to be provided for each cresset. One carried the cresset, and the other bore fuel to keep it alight. Each man, in addition to his wages, received a straw hat with a badge painted, and his breakfast in the morning. The cressets are thus noticed by an old poet :—

> "   .   .   .   Let nothing that's magnifical,
> Or that may tend to London's graceful state,
> Be unperformed, as showes and solemn feasts,
> Watches in armour, triumphs, cresset lights,
> Bonfires, bells, and peals of ordnance,
> And pleasure."

In old pageants, cressets were generally used to

give a light to the proceedings. The cresset consisted of an open pan hanging upon swivels, fastened to an iron forked staff. The pan contained burning pitch, or other combustibles.

Hone, in his " Every-Day Book," has some informing and interesting notes on cressets. " When the cresset light was stationary," remarks Hone, " it served as a beacon, or answered the purpose of a fixed lamp, and in this way our ancestors illuminated or lighted up their streets. There is a volume of sermons, by Samuel Ward, printed 1617-24, with a wood-cut frontispiece, representing two of these fixed cressets or street-lamps, with verses between them, in relation to his name and character as a faithful watchman. In the first lines old Ward is addressed thus : —

> ' *Watch* WARD, and keepe thy Garments tight,
> For I come thiefe-like at Midnight.'

Whereunto Ward answers the injunction to *watch* in the lines following :—

> ' All seeing, never-slumbering LORD :
> Be thou my *Watch*, I'll be thy WARD.'"

Henry VIII., in 1539, caused the annual pageant on Midsummer-night to be discontinued. The assigned reason for this step was the great expense of the ceremony. A few years later, namely in 1548, during the mayoralty of Sir Thomas Gresham, the custom was revived. Twenty years later the marching watch and procession were re-modelled, and a standing watch, at much less cost, was instituted.

The annual ceremonies connected with the Watch were not peculiar to London, for some of the larger provincial towns had their imposing customs. At the city of Chester, on St. John's Eve, for example, there was much pomp and pageantry. In an ordinance of the Mayor, Aldermen, and Common Councilmen of the city, dated 1564, and preserved among the Harleian MSS., in the British Museum, the pageant is referred to as "according to ancient custom." It is directed that the following appear in the procession : four giants, one unicorn, one dromedary, one camel, one luce, one dragon, and six hobby-horses, with other figures. In 1599, the mayor, Henry Hardware, caused the giants to be broken, and in their place was substituted a man clad in complete armour. Two years later, another mayor reinstated the giants. During the Commonwealth the show was discontinued, and the beasts and giants destroyed. At the Restoration the citizens of Chester re-

organised their ancient custom, had new models
made, and produced a pageant worthy of the old
traditions of the place.

Nottingham is another town celebrated for its
quaint ceremonies respecting setting the watch
on Midsummer Eve.   Deering, the local historian,
in his *Nottinghamia Vetus et Nova*, published in
1751, reproduces from an old authority a curious
account of the custom.   " Every inhabitant," says
Deering, " of any ability sets forth a man, as well
voluntaries as those who are charged with arms,
with such munition as they have ; some pikes,
some muskets, calivers, or other guns ; some
partisans or halberds ; and such as have armour
send their servants in their armour.   The number
of these are yearly almost two hundred, who at
sun-set meet in the Row, the most open part of
the town, where the Mayor's serjeant-at-mace
gives them an oath, the tenor whereof followeth
in these words : ' You shall well and truly keep
this town till to-morrow at the sun-rising.   You
shall come unto no house without license, or cause
reasonable.   Of all manner of casualties ; of fire,
of crying of children, you shall due warning make
to the parties, as the case shall require.   You
shall due search make of all manner of affrays,

bloodsheds, outcrys, and all other things that be suspected,' etc. Which done, they all march in orderly array through the principal streets of the town, and then they are sorted into several companies, and designed to several parts of the town, where they are to keep watch until the sun dismisses them in the morning. In this business the fashion is for every watchman to wear a garland, made in the fashion of a crown imperial, bedecked with flowers of various kinds, some natural, some artificial, bought and kept for the purpose, as also ribbands, jewels, and for the better garnishing whereof the townsmen use the day before to ransack the gardens of all the gentlemen within six or seven miles round Nottingham, besides what the town itself affords them : their greatest ambition being to out-do one another in the bravery of their garlands." The custom was kept up till the days of Charles I.

During the thirty-eight years reign of Henry VIII. much was done to try and check the lawless life of the people. In his reign, according to Stow, not fewer than 72,000 great thieves, petty thieves, and rogues were executed. London, at this period, remained a dangerous place after nightfall. Instead of the marching watch, sturdy constables, well armed, were appointed. They were provided with lanterns, and carried halberds, or other formidable weapons. These men were not to be trifled with.

We gather from Stow that, in the days of Queen Mary, a bellman was instituted in each

BELLMEN, TEMP. QUEEN MARY.

ward. These men during the long nights wandered through the streets and lanes of London, saluting their masters and mistresses with suitable rhymes for the season of the year, and at the same time bidding them to hang out their lights. The usage was in accordance with a rule made in 1416, when Sir Henry Barton was the Mayor of London. He ordered, says Charles Knight, "lanterns and lights to be hanged out in the winter evenings betwixt Allhallows and Candlemas. For three centuries this practice subsisted, constantly evaded, no doubt, through the avarice and poverty of the individuals, sometimes probably disused altogether, but still the custom of London up to the time of Queen Anne."

Attempts were made to preserve silence in the streets in Queen Elizabeth's time. We gather from the "Statutes of the Streets" of her reign, that men were prescribed from blowing horns or whistles after nine o'clock at night, under pain of imprisonment. These regulations forbade "a man to make any sudden outcry in the still of the night, as making any affray, or beating his wife."

Under the portrait of a watchman in the days of James I., are the following lines :—

> "A light here, maids, hang out your lights,
> And see that your horns be clear and bright,
> That so your candle clear may shine,
> Continuing from six till nine ;
> That honest men that walk along
> May see to pass safe without wrong."

A work entitled the " Pleasant Concerts of Old

Hobson, the Merry Londoner," 1606, contains the following droll story :—"When the order of hanging out lanterne and candlelight first of all was brought up, the bedell of the warde where Maister Hobson dwelt, in a darke evening, crieing up and down, 'Hang out your lanternes !' 'Hang out your lanternes !' using no other wordes, Maister Hobson tooke emptie lanterne, and according to the bedell's call, hung it out. This flout by the Lord Mayor was taken in ill part, and for the same offence Hobson was sent to the Counter; but being released the next night following, thinking to amend his call, the bedell cried out with a loud voice, 'Hang out your lanternes and candles !' Maister Hobson thereupon hung out a lanterne unlighted, as the bedell again commanded ; whereupon he was again sent to the Counter; but the next night, the bedell, being better advised, cryed 'Hang out your lanterne and candlelight !' which Maister Hobson at last did, to his great commendation, which cry of lanterne and candlelight is in right manner used to this day."

It will be noticed from a picture of a watchman in the time of James I., that he was a man venerable in appearance, and was perhaps

selected from the feeble folk in order to keep him
from being a burden on the parish. Above the
head of the man, in the original picture from
which our cut is copied, there is a copy of the cry
which he uttered when going his nightly rounds.
It is this : " Lanthorne and a whole candell light,
hange out your lights heare !"

The old watchmen appear to have gone from bad

to worse, until watch
and ward were little
better than a farce.
The introduction of
Peel's policemen, in
1829, was a much
needed institution.
Prior to this period
men unable to work
and obliged to apply

WATCHMAN, TEMP. JAMES I.

to the parish for relief were usually appointed
watchmen. The truth of this statement is
borne out by a writer in the *Morning Herald*,
of October 30th, 1802 : — " It is said that
a man who presented himself for the office of
watchman to a parish at the West-end of the
town, very much infested by depredators, was
lately turned away from the vestry with this

reprimand: 'I am astonished at the impudence of such a great, sturdy, strong fellow as you, being so idle as to apply for a Watchman's situation, when you are capable of labour!'" The outfit of these superannuated paupers consisted of a lantern, rattle, staff, and treble-caped great-coat. He had a small wooden box placed against the wall to retire into in case of rain and storm, but in which he usually snored away the night. The watchman, lantern in hand, to light his lonely path, would, with tottering steps, go round his beat, "announcing the hour as clearly as a husky cough of some ten years' standing would admit." He

WATCHMAN IN HIS BOX.

would proclaim: "Pa-a-ast ten o'clock, and a rai-ny night!" "Past two o'clock, and a cloudy mo——orning!"

The old watchmen were known as "Charlies." They afforded much enjoyment for the "bloods"

and " bucks " of the period. It was a favourite
form of diversion for them to torment the watchman. If they caught one asleep, which was by
no means infrequent, they would overturn his box,
or turn the door to the wall, leaving the sleepy
occupant to get it right the best way he could when
he awoke. Sometimes the watchmen would turn
on their tormentors, when often fractured heads
and broken arms would result.

Few of the old watch-boxes remain ; not long
ago we saw one at Salford, Lancashire.

Under Lock and Key.

IN the olden time, the gates of towns were
locked at an early hour at night, and no
persons were permitted to enter or leave after
closing time. The custom dates back to an early
period in our history, and has given rise to not a
few romantic episodes.

Exeter records supply a most tragical tale of
the days of Edward I. His wise legislation
gained for him the title of "the English Justinian."
He was, however, extremely severe. During
one year of his reign, namely in 1279, two
hundred and eighty Jews were hanged for
clipping coin. Little regard was felt by him
for human life. In 1285, at the solicita-
tion of Quivil, the Bishop of Exeter, he visited
Exeter to enquire into the circumstances relating
to the assassination of Walter Lichdale, a precentor of the cathedral, who had been killed one
day when returning from matins. The murderer
made his escape during the night, and could not
be found. The Mayor, Alfred Dunport, who had
held the office on eight occasions, and the porter

c

of the South gate, were both tried, and found
guilty of a neglect of duty in omitting to fasten
the town gate, by which means the murderer
escaped from the hands of justice.   Both men
were   condemned   to   death,   and   afterwards
executed.   The unfortunate mayor and porter
had not anything to do with the death of the
precentor, their only crime being that of not closing the city gate at night.   Truly a hard fate for
neglect of duty.

The chief authorities of towns in past ages
incurred much responsibility.   At Ripon we have
a good example of their liabilities.   Here formerly,
after the blowing of a horn at nine o'clock at
night, and until sunrise next morning, if a house
was robbed, and the owner and his servants had
taken proper precautions for its safety, the wake-
man had to make good the loss sustained.   Each
householder paid an annual tax of twopence if he
had one door, and fourpence if he had two
doors to his dwelling, for maintaining a watch
over the city.   The tax has long since been discontinued, but the horn is still blown at night.   It
is said that the custom dates back to the days of
our Anglo-Saxon ancestors.

As might be expected, the history of York

embraces many important passages on this subject. It was the old practice when a king visited the city, to lend to him the keys of the city gates, and when he departed he gave them up.

In past ages, it was customary to fix on spikes, over the city gates, the heads of persons beheaded for high treason, etc. At York have figured the heads of some famous men. On the 30th December, 1460, was fought the battle of Wakefield, and there was slain the Duke of York. Lord Clifford ordered his head to be cut off, and presented to Queen Margaret, who, it is said, caused to be placed on it in derision a paper crown. It was subsequently fixed on a spike over Micklegate Bar, York, as a warning to his adherents.

The citizens of York feared trouble after the battle of Bosworth-field. They had supported the fallen monarch, and could expect little favour from the successful Richmond. At a meeting held on the 31st August, 1485, in the Council Chamber, and presided over by the Lord Mayor, it was determined to close all the city gates at nine o'clock in the evening, and open them at four o'clock in the morning. Four men from each ward in the city were appointed to watch at the gates every night.

Great precaution used to be taken against the Scotch in the North of England. Many were the battles between the men of England and Scotland. A Scotchman was not formerly permitted to enter the city of York without a license

BOOTHAM BAR, YORK.

from the Lord Mayor, the Warden, or the Constable, on pain of imprisonment. In 1501, hammers were placed on each of the Bars for Scotchmen to knock before entering.

Elias Micklethwaite filled the office of chief magistrate of York in the year 1615, and during his mayoralty he attempted to enforce a strict observance of the Sabbath. During the Sunday, he kept the city gates closed, and thus prevented the inhabitants from going into the country for pleasure.

On two critical occasions in the national history, the gates of Hull have been closed. Boling-broke, Duke of Lancaster, afterwards King Henry IV., landed, July 4, 1399, at Ravenspurne, in Holderness, a port long since washed away by the sea. There he was joined by a number of discontented noblemen, the chief being the Percies, of Northumberland, who were determined to depose King Richard II. News of the warlike movements soon reached Hull, and John Tut-bury, the mayor, directed the bridges to be drawn up, and the gates to be shut. He placed the burgesses under arms, and prepared for action, if required. The duke and his followers ap-proached the town, and demanded immediate admission. The mayor refused, saying "that he had sworn to be true to his sovereign, Richard II., and faithfully to keep the town for his use, and that he fully intended to do his duty, and never prove false to his oath, and a traitor to his king." On receiving this loyal and resolute reply, the duke retired, and made his way to Doncaster.

The closing of the gates of Hull against Charles I., in the year 1642, was an act of great importance, and was most favourable to the

SIR JOHN HOTHAM.

Parliamentary party. The king, at the outset of the struggle between himself and the Parliament, repaired to Hull, which possessed the best magazine of munitions of war in the country

He expected a welcome in the loyal borough, which had been greatly favoured by the kings of England, but to his great surprise and disappointment, Sir John Hotham, the governor of the town, shut the gates against him. The king had to retire to York discomfited. Parliament thanked Sir John for the bold stand made on the trying occasion. His subsequent career was very sad. He felt slighted when Lord Fairfax was entrusted with the generalship of the North, believing that the position was one to which he was entitled. On refusing to obey the orders of Fairfax, he was removed from his governorship. In a jealous pique, he decided to transfer his services to the king, and deliver the town into his hands. The plot was discovered, and Hotham had to fly. On reaching Beverley, he was apprehended by his nephew, Captain Boynton, and carried back to Hull, thence to London, where he was tried with his son for "traitorously betraying the trust reposed in them by Parliament," found guilty, and beheaded on Tower Hill.

We find in the "Autobiographic Recollections of George Pryme," a note showing how closely the town was guarded in past times. Writing of the years 1781-1796, he states, "Hull was formerly enclosed, partly by water, and partly by walls. In my grandfather's time, the gates were closed at ten o'clock at night, and could not be passed without an order, which rule was so rigidly enforced that my great aunt (his sister), who

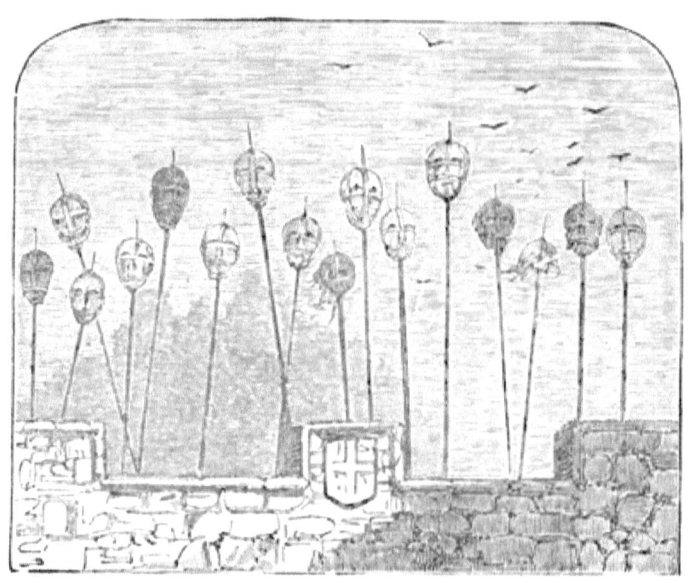

HEADS OF TRAITORS ON A CITY GATE.

resided a little out of the town, used on evenings of the assemblies to sleep at her brother's house."

At the city of Carlisle were three gates, known as the English, Irish, and Scotch gates, on account of opening towards the three kingdoms. A cannon was formerly fired at night to warn those without that required ingress, to enter without delay, and those who wished to leave the city to depart at once. The gates when once closed remained shut until sunrise next morning. Over the gates were displayed the heads of rebels. An old lady from Dumfriesshire related to Allan Cunningham the terror she experienced at seeing the heads of her countrymen there exposed to view. Respecting one of the heads, that of a comely youth with long yellow hair, a pathetic story is told, and adds romance to the local history. "A young and beautiful lady," so runs the tale, "came every morning at sunrise, and every evening at sunset, to look at the head of the yellow-haired laddie, till at length both lady and head disappeared. The incident is commemorated in a song, in which the sick-hearted damsel bewails the fate of her lover." A couple of verses are as follow :

> "White was the rose in my love's hat
> As he rowed me in his lowland plaidie ;
> His heart was true as death in love,
> His hand was aye in battle ready.

> "His long, long hair, in yellow hanks,
> Wav'd o'er his cheeks sae sweet and ruddy ;
> But now it waves o'er Carlisle yetts
> In dripping ringlets, soil'd and bloody."

At the rebellion of 1745, when the Highland

soldiers were passing southward, they did not enter Carlisle by the Scotch gate, on which "the grim and ghastly heads of their brethren were exhibited."

Villages as well as towns had their gates, which were closed at night. It is believed that the retired village of Eyam, Derbyshire, was one of the last places in the country to give up the old custom. The chief road to this out-of-the-way place is called the Ligget—a name derived from the Saxon word Lyd, or Lid, signifying to cover or protect. From a remote time down to about a century ago, a strong gate was closed at nightfall, and guarded until morning. " Every effective man," says William Wood, "who was a householder in the village, was bound to stand in succession at this gate from nine o'clock at night till six in the morning to question any person who might appear at the gate wishing for entrance into the village, and to give alarm if danger were apprehended. The watchman had a large wooden halbert, or 'watch-bill,' for protection, and when he came off watch in the morning he took the 'watch-bill' and reared it against the door of the person whose turn to watch succeeded his ; and so on in succession."

From a very early period the keeping of the North gate, one of the most important gates in Chester, was held on the curious condition " of seeing the extreme sentence of the law executed on malefactors, whether condemned by the city or county courts." Hemingway's " History of Chester " contains much information on this subject, and corrects some of the fabulous stories respecting the origin of the custom. " It is stated," says the historian, " in an inquisition taken in the year 1321, for the purpose of ascertaining the tolls payable at each of the city gates, that the mayor and citizens, as keepers of the North gate, had a right to certain tolls, for which privilege they were bound to watch the said gate, and prisoners in the prison ; to keep the key of the felon's gallows ; to hang up all condemned criminals ; to execute the sentence of the pillory, etc." Other items of more or less interest are mentioned.

The annals of Winchester include not a few passages of importance bearing on this theme. The country people, it is stated, who brought their waggons and carts to the market had to pay a penny toll to the king for passing through the city gates. They entered by three of the gates, and a

fourth was used by foot-passengers and horsemen. We gather from a quotation in " Historic
Winchester " that " In the forty-third year of
Henry III., the prior and monks of S. Swithun's
blocked up three gates so that the king lost the
toll. The sheriff of the county and the bailiffs of
the city were ordered to remove the obstructions
to these gates, but were met by certain monks
(amongst them one called Roger le Diable) and
lay brothers, in ecclesiastical vestments, with
lighted tapers, who publicly excommunicated the
royal officers. This having been deposed on
oath, it was ordered that all the lands and tene-
ments of the prior and convent should be taken
into the king's hands." This commotion occurred
in the year 1259.

A plague ravaged England in the year 1603,
and 36,000 perished by it. An attempt was made
to keep it out of Winchester. A strict watch was
kept at the city gates, and suspicious persons
were dismissed from the town.

Respecting stopping Beverley people at the
gates of Hull, the following indignant letter was
sent from Beverley in 1633 :

" Sir,— [This] forenoone came unexpected tidings of a stop
of our towne's people [at] your Gates, upon a false report con-

cerning a fresh breaking out of [the] plague at Mr. Cawthorp's house (which was first infected). Wee did [hope] you would not have credited any such, not haveing received any report from US to that purpose ; our towne, blessed bee God, is in a very safe and good condition, and soe are all the persons in the Pesthouse, whome wee are very shortly to set at large, being now about to clense the house. [   ] you will please to enquire of the origional of this report. [If any] of your towne bee culpable, 'tis fit they should bee severely [punished], wich I hope you will doe ; in confidence whereof I take Leave.
—Your affec'conate freind and servant,

"EDWD. GREY, Major.

"[Indorsed—These for the Right worshipful the Mayor of Kingston upon Hull, Prsent.]"

Four years later, the gates of Beverley were closed against the residents of Hull. In 1637 the plague raged in Hull, and the members of the Beverley Corporation did their utmost to prevent the introduction of the contagion into their town. It was resolved not to permit any concourse of people to assemble. An order set forth "that upon woman's occasions, as childe bearing or christenings and the like ther shall not bee above ten persones at once, and those bee the especial friends and neighbours, under pain of 20s. to be forfeited by the partie that causeth the meeting." No person, says the local historian, Sheahan, in some notes drawn from the town records, was allowed "to receive any goods from Hull, as linen clothes, wool, or woollen, or anie other goods, upon payne of forfeiture of £5, of lawful English monie, for each offence." And it was also decreed " that no manner of persons within the towne of Beverley shall resort unto the said towne of Kingstone, for any commerce whatsoever, without the license of Mr. Mair and two Governors at leaste, upon payne of 10s., to be levied by distress, and for want of distress to bee imprisoned for three days, and then fined sureties for good behaviour." We are further told that if any inhabitant of Beverley entertained any inhabitant of Hull, without a certificate from the mayor of Hull, and the approbation of the mayor of Beverley, and two of the governors, at least, of the same town, the person so offending forfeited £5.

The Practice of Pledging.

THE custom of pledging has come down to us from a remote period in our history. Few of us as we perform the ceremony at the festive board call to remembrance the old historical associations connected with it.

It is generally agreed that the word "pledge" is derived from the French *pleige*, a surety or gage. According to some authorities, we derive the saying "I'll pledge you" from a practice instituted in the days when the Danes were in power in this country. We are told it was no uncommon occurrence for the treacherous invaders to invite the Saxons with whom they came in contact to drink with them, and while drinking to plunge a knife or a dagger into their throats. It came to pass that a man would not drink with a stranger until someone undertook to give a pledge for his safety. The pledger then held up his knife or sword to protect the person drinking. An unprotected man was an easy victim for a foe when engaged in the act of drinking.

Shakespeare, in his *Timon of Athens*, act 1., scene 5, has the following passage referring to the pledging of the Danes :—

> ".   .   .   .   .   .   .   If I
> Were a huge man I should fear to drink at meals,
> Lest they should spy my windpipe's dangerous notes,
> Great men should drink *with harness on their throats.*"

The Rev. Robert Henry, D.D., wrote a "History of Great Britain" in several volumes, and the second was issued in 1774. In that volume are some curious notes on this subject. "If an Englishman," says Henry, "presumed to drink in the presence of a Dane without express permission, it was esteemed a great mark of disrespect, that nothing but his instant death could expiate. Nay, the English were so intimidated that they would not adventure to drink even when they were invited, until the Danes had pledged their honour for their safety. The man who pledged the drinker stood by weapon in hand to protect him."

It is generally believed that young Edward the Martyr was, in 979, assassinated at the instigation of his false-hearted step-mother, the infamous Elfrida. He was stabbed in the back while drinking a stirrup-cup at Corfe Castle. The object of the murder was to place Elfrida's son on the throne. It is asserted by some writers that from this tragedy we derive the custom of pledging.

The Danes drank to an immoderate extent, and their example had a baneful effect upon the English. King Edgar, acting under the advice of Dunstan, the Archbishop of Canterbury, put down many ale-houses, and only permitted one for each small town or village. He also invented the famous "peg-tankards." In these tankards pins or nails were fastened at certain distances, and it was the law that "whosoever should drink beyond these marks at one draught should be liable to a severe punishment." The law appears to have given rise to a custom known as "Pin-drinking, or nick the pin," an explanation of which is given in "Cocker's Dictionary":—
"Pin-drinking.—An old way of drinking exactly to a pin in the midst of a wooden cup, which being somewhat difficult, occasioned much drunkenness; so a law was made that priests, monks, and friars should not drink to or at the pins." It would appear from the preceding note that the usage had the opposite effect to the laudable intention of Edgar.

Some curious notes are contained in Barrington's

"Observations on the Ancient Statutes" (published 1775), which are well worth reproducing. "It was anciently the custom," says Barrington, "for a person swearing fealty to hold his hands joined together between those of his lord ; the reason of which seems to have been that some lord had been assassinated under pretence of paying homage, but, while the tenant's hands continued in this attitude, it was impossible for him to make such an attempt. I take the same reason to have occasioned the ceremony still adhered to by the scholars in Queen's College, at Oxford, who wait upon the fellows placing their thumbs upon the table ; which, as I have been informed, still continues in some parts of Germany whilst the superior drinks the health of the inferior. The suspicion that men formerly had of attempts upon their lives on such occasions is well known, and forms the common account with regard to the origin." Perhaps, after all, the best explanation of the origin of a custom which prevails among all peoples, and in all ages, is the one that sees in it a natural instinct, common, indeed, to animals and men.

The works of the old poets contain many references to pledging and kindred matters. In

Beaumont and Fletcher's time we are told that it was customary for the young gallants to stab themselves in the arms or elsewhere, so that in their own blood they could drink the healths or write the names of their mistresses. In the "Oxford Drollery," published in 1671, is an allusion to the usage :—

> *"I stab'd mine arm to drink her health,*
>   The more fool I, the more fool I ;
> I will no more her servant be,
>   The wiser I, the wiser I,
> *Nor pledge her health upon my knee."*

The Minstrel in the Olden Time.

"Many a carol old and saintly
Sang the minstrels and the waits."

THE minstrel comes on the scene at an early period in the annals of England. The bards of the ancient Britons composed poems in praise of heroic deeds, and sang their songs to the strains of the lyre. They won the affection of the highest and lowest in the land. Their music and poetry added refinement to the rude everyday life of our remote ancestors. It is asserted by some of the chroniclers, that the influence of the bards was so great that even when armies were on the point of battle they would walk in the front of the warriors and sing songs, with such strange power as to cause swords to be sheathed and an engagement to be avoided.

The Anglo-Saxons had their gleemen, who were favourites at the Court of the King, and at the houses of the nobility. They chanted to the notes of the harp "tales of love and war, romance and knightly worth." Not only were these wandering musicians received as honoured guests at the stately halls, but they were permitted to enter unmolested into hostile camps in the time of war. Every reader of our history is familiar with the story of Alfred the Great going into the Danish camp as a spy, in the guise of a harper, and so delighting Guthrum, the general, with music and song that he rewarded him in a liberal manner, and pressed him to remain. In a few days Alfred learned all he wanted to know, for the Danes spoke freely before him, whom they only regarded as a poor wandering musician. The knowledge obtained he turned to good account, and in the next battle with the Danish foes he defeated them, and resumed the rule of the country.

Saxon gleemen, besides playing musical instruments and singing songs, danced and performed juggling and other antics. Some of them, as early as the tenth century, devoted attention to training animals to dance, tumble, and act a variety of tricks at command. The Saxons played on several instruments, including the psaltery of various shapes, lyre, viol, cymbals, flute, harp, organ, sambuca, small bells, etc.

The Saxons were great lovers of music, and

we gather from Bede's notice of the poet Cædmon, "that it was usual at their feasts to pass the harp round from hand to hand, and every man was supposed to be able to sing in his turn, and accompany himself on the instrument."

In tracing the history of minstrels under the Normans, we find an account of the heroic conduct of Taillefer, a warrior and musician, who came to England with William the Conqueror. "He was," says Strutt, "present at the battle of Hastings, and appeared at the head of the Conqueror's army, singing the songs of Charlemagne, and of Roland; but previous to the commencement of the action, he advanced on horseback towards the army of the English, and casting his spear three times into the air, he caught it as often by the iron head; and the fourth time he threw it among his enemies, one of whom he wounded in the body; he then drew his sword, which he also tossed in the air as many times as he had done his spear, and caught it with such dexterity that those who saw him attributed his manœuvres to the power of enchantment." At the conclusion of the feat, Strutt states, "he galloped among the English soldiers, thereby giving the Normans the signal of battle ; and in the action it appears he lost his life."

The minstrels who flourished in this country under the Norman rule, embraced rhymers, singers, story-tellers, jugglers, relaters of heroic actions, buffoons, and poets. It is related that "the courts of the princes swarmed with poets and minstrels. The earls also, the great barons, who in their castles emulated the pomp of royalty, had their poets and minstrels ; they formed part of their household establishment, and, exclusive of their wages, were provided with board, lodging, and clothing by their patrons, and frequently travelled with them when they went from home." The chief towns had their minstrels, who were usually called waits. These men were really musical watchmen, parading the streets and singing the hour of the night, and intimating the state of the weather. They proclaimed the time thus : " Two o'clock, and a fine frosty morning." This custom was kept up by the old watchmen in our larger towns until the introduction of the police by Sir Robert Peel. Some of the town minstrels were banded together in gilds, and in not a few instances were persons of wealth and importance. The fraternity at Beverley, York-

shire, was one of great antiquity, its members were
men of means, and they are frequently named in
the records of the town.   In the reign of Henry
VI., they gave one of the pillars to St. Mary's
Church, and on the capital of it is sculptured a
representation of the band of minstrels.   Over
the figures is the following inscription :—*Thys
Pyllor made the meynstyrls;* and on the trans-
verse side :—*Orate pro animabus pro Hysteriorum.*
The figures, which are five in number, are somewhat damaged, but a good idea of their costume
and musical instruments may be gathered from a
study of them.   We reproduce from Carter's
" Ancient Painting and Sculpture," a capital cut of
the minstrels.   The centre carving is that of the
Alderman, or the chief of the band.   He is
pictured in a tight jacket of tawny colour, over
which is a loose coat, with wide sleeves, and
round his neck is a chain.   The others also wear
chains ; some have tassels and pouches at their
sides, but not loose overcoats.   The sculpture is
highly coloured.   The historian of Beverley, Mr.
George Poulson, writing in 1829, says : " The
following are the original colours in which they
were painted, before they were disfigured with the
present colouring :—the belt, tassels, and badges,

blue ; chains, yellow ; pouches, blue ; stockings, black or brown ; shirt waist, white or buff ; viol, blue ; harp, blue ; pipe, brown ; and the hair, black." In the town accounts for the year 1460, there are entries for red wine, etc., given to twenty armed men, and it is stated, "also paid to three minstrels of the town for their labour at the time of the passage of the said armed men out of the town,

THE BEVERLEY MINSTRELS.

sixpence." There is an item in 1502, for a payment "for nine ells of tawny cloth bought and given to the minstrels for their clothing this year, one shilling." In the same year, another entry states that a shilling was "given to the minstrels at Crossgarths to drink in rogation days."

The oldest document̄on this subject which has come down to us is a copy of the minstrels' laws of the time of Queen Mary, 1555. The rules are similar to the regulations which governed the old trade gilds. The preamble of the document states that it has been the custom since the days of King Athelstan for the minstrels living between the rivers Trent and Tweed to annually meet at Beverley at rogation days for the election of an alderman, stewards, and deputies, for admitting new members, collecting fees, and transacting the other business of the fraternity. A copy of the ancient regulations may be read in Poulson's " History of Beverley."

Chester was the headquarters of another famous band of minstrels. Ranulph, the Earl of Chester, granted to the Duttons authority over the minstrels of his jurisdiction. Dugdale gives details of curious customs of the Chester minstrels which lasted down to his day. Referring to Chester Midsummer Fair, he writes, "all the minstrels of the county resorting to Chester, do attend the heir of Dutton from his lodging to St. John's Church (he being then accompanied by many gentlemen of the county) ; one of the minstrels walking before him in a surcoat of his arms, depicted on taffeta, the rest of his fellows proceeding two and two, and playing on their several sorts of musical instruments.

And after divine service ended, gave the like attendance on him back to his lodgings, where, the court being kept by his (Mr. Dutton's) steward, and all the minstrels formally called, certain orders and laws are usually made for the better government of the society ; with penalties on those that transgress." The other facts are of greater local than general interest, and may be found in the histories of Chester.

John of Gaunt, Duke of Lancaster, was a liberal patron of music, doubtless the greatest amongst his countrymen. It will be remembered that he was the friend, and by marriage a kinsman, of Chaucer. We may infer from the frequent allusions to the minstrels' arts in Chaucer's pages, that he delighted in their performances. John of Gaunt lived in Tutbury Castle in regal splendour. After the death of his first wife, he wedded the Princess Constance, and by the right of this union, assumed the title of King of Castile and Leon. The devoted pair were lovers of music, which made merry their mansion. In the reign of the second Richard, in the year 1377, John of Gaunt founded a Minstrels' Court at Tutbury. It was presided over by a King of Minstrels, who had the entire control over the musicians of no less than five counties. On the morrow after the Assumption, a large gathering of minstrels met at Tutbury, and marched in procession to the parish church. The King walked with stately tread, and on either side of him were the bailiff of the manor and the steward of the court. He was also attended by four other stewards belonging to the court, bearing white wands to denote their office. They returned in the same order to the Castle Hall, where the King took his seat, supported by the bailiff and steward.

The next business was the opening of the court by proclamation, directing to draw near and give attendance all minstrels residing within the honour of Tutbury, either in the counties of Derby, Stafford, Nottingham, Warwick, or Lancaster; and it was stated that pleas would be heard, and fines and amercements made. After the court roll had been called over, two juries were empanelled and charged. " The jurors then," says Mr. Llewellynn Jewitt, who has compiled some notes on this subject, " proceeded to the selection of officers for the ensuing year. The jurors having left the court for the purpose, the King and stewards partook of a banquet, while the

musicians played their best on their respective
instruments. On the return of the jurors, they
presented the new King, whom they had chosen
from the four stewards; upon which the old King
rising, delivered to him his wand of office, and
drank a cup of wine to his health and prosperity.
In like manner the old stewards saluted and
resigned their office to their successors. This
ended, the court rose, and adjourned to a general
banquet in another part of the castle." Some
sports followed, the chief amusement being the
running of a mad bull. Previous to being let
loose, the bull's horns were sawed off close to the
head, and the tail cut off to the stump, next it
was covered with grease, and to infuriate it still
further, its nostrils were filled with pepper.
"While these preparations were being made,"
observes Mr. Jewitt, "the steward made proclamation that all manner of persons should
give way to the bull, no person coming nearer to
it than forty feet, except the minstrels, but that
all should attend to their own safety, everyone at
his peril. The bull being then turned out, was to
be caught by someone of the minstrels, and no one
else, between that hour and sunset on the same
day, within the county of Stafford. If he escaped

he remained the property of the person who gave it, formerly the Prior of Tutbury ; but if any of the minstrels could lay hold of him so as to cut off a portion of the hair and bring it to the Market Cross, he was caught and taken to the bailiff, by whom he was fastened to a rope, etc., and then brought to the bull-ring in High Street, where he was baited by dogs. After this the minstrels could either sell or divide him amongst themselves." This brutal pastime prevailed down to the year 1778, when happily it was stopped. The custom was known as Tutbury-day, and in Robin Hood Ballads and other old songs and poems it is mentioned.

The King of the Minstrels was not a title confined to Tutbury. The reigning monarchs designated their head minstrel as King, and he travelled with his royal master, directing the sports and engaging other minstrels belonging to the household.

In 1415, Henry V. took with him to France a company of eighteen minstrels. It is recorded that in 1456 "an ordinance was passed for the impressment of youths to supply vacancies by death amongst the king's minstrels." These musicians were popular down to the reign of

Henry VIII. On the 1st of July, 1541, a Welsh minstrel suffered death for singing a prophecy against the king. After this period they attracted little attention, and during the visit of Elizabeth to Kenilworth Castle, in 1575, the attendance of a minstrel created much surprise. The end of the minstrel's art came in 1597, when an Act was passed which included them amongst "rogues, vagabonds, and sturdy beggars, and adjudged them to be punished accordingly."

Sir Walter Scott draws a graphic picture of the last of the Border minstrels. The date of his poem, "The Lay of the Last Minstrel," is about the middle of the sixteenth century.

"The minstrel," we are told, "was infirm and old."

> "Old times have changed, old manners gone,
> A stranger filled the Stuart's throne ;
> The bigots of the iron time
> Had called his harmless art a crime,
> A wandering harper, scorned and poor,
> He begged his bread from door to door ;
> And tuned, to please a peasant's ear,
> The harp a King had loved to hear."

Curious Landholding Customs.

IN bygone times jocular tenures and mirthful manorial customs formed a curious feature of land-holding in England, and these old-time usages supplied a close link between the king and the baron, and between the baron and the vassal. It is in some instances difficult to see the utility of many of the quaint ceremonies, but we may safely rest assured that they were well adapted for the age in what they were enacted.

Fighting was the business of a baron's life in feudal times. He often received for his services extensive grants of land, and held them on condition of furnishing men and horses in the time of war, or for performing services more or less military in their character. We can readily realise how expedient it was to compel holders of land to help in the time of trouble. In the days of old the sword was almost the only means of keeping possession of the throne, and bearing this in mind we may easily conceive the importance of instituting tenures, which were the means of providing men ready to take the field for king and country.

There were two classes of crown tenures, one called *grand sergeanty*, and the other *petit sergeanty*. In the former, personal service had to be rendered to the king, and this was regarded as the most honourable of tenures. It consisted of assisting at the king's coronation, bearing his banner, or his spear, or some such service. The yielding to the king annually, but not in person, towards his wars, a sword, dagger, bow, spurs, and the like, was the service of *petit serjeanty*.

William the Conqueror granted large lots of land to Robert de Marmyon on condition that he and his heirs filled the office of king's champion. The male line of the family closed in the year 1292, and by marriage the championship passed to the Dymokes. At the coronation of the English monarchs, from the time of Richard II. to the days of George IV., a period extending over nearly four and a half centuries, the representative of the Dymokes rode into Westminster Hall at the coronation feast during the dinner, between the first and second course, mounted on one of the king's horses, and clad in one of the king's best suits of armour, and there and then challenged any one to gainsay the right of his majesty to the throne. At the coronation of William IV., the champion was supported on the right and left by the Duke of Wellington and the Marquis of Aylesbury. A herald read the following challenge :—

" If any person, of what degree soever, high or low, shall deny or gainsay our Sovereign Lord, George the Fourth, of the United Kingdom of Great Britain and Ireland, Defender of the Faith, Son and next Heir to our Sovereign Lord, King George the Third, deceased, to be the right Heir to the Imperial Crown of the United Kingdom, or that he ought not to enjoy the same, here is his Champion, who saith that he lieth, and is a false traitor ; being ready in person to combat with him, and in this quarrel will venture his life against him, on what day soever shall be appointed."

The words are almost similar to those used at the coronation of Richard II. After the challenge had been given, Dymoke defiantly threw down his gauntlet. After remaining on the floor for a short time it was picked up by a herald and returned to him. The ceremony was

THE CHAMPION.

enacted three times, once on entering the hall,
next in the middle of the hall, and lastly at the
foot of the throne. The king drank to the health
of his champion out of a gold cup, which was then
passed to him and retained. In addition to the
cup, he also kept the horse on which he rode, and
the suit of armour which he wore.

Services in connection with coronations were
numerous and often curious. At Addington,
Surrey, in the days of Henry III., was granted a
tract of land on consideration that the holder of
it prepared one mess in the kitchen on the day
the king was crowned. Lands were held by
others by taking charge of the king's table-cloths,
and finding a spit of maple to roast the king's
meat on the day of coronation. The manor of
Stapleton, in the parish of Martock, was held by
the service of holding a towel before the Queen,
at the coronation of her husband, and also at the
feasts of Easter, Whitsuntide, and Christmas.
Henry VIII. made in 1542 an important
grant to a son of the Earl of Shrewsbury. It
consisted of a lot of land in the parish of
Worksop, Nottinghamshire. In return for the
land he had to provide a right-hand glove for
the king and support his right arm during

the time he held the sceptre. This service is still performed.

Land was granted to an Atfield, of Allerton, for attending on the king when he crossed the Channel, and holding the head of his Majesty if he were sea-sick. One man held his estate on condition that he personally presented himself in the king's chamber whenever his company was wanted.

In the olden time, even kings reclined on beds of straw. Blount gives particulars of a provision for providing straw for the beds of our earlier Norman kings. Land was held at Aylesbury on condition of finding straw for the bed of our lord the king, and for strewing his chamber with straw when he visited Aylesbury in winter. In summer, straw had to be provided for the bed, and grass or rushes for the bedroom floor. The service had only to be performed three times a year if the king visited the town.

A tenure entailing much trouble was attached to Shirefield, Hants. The lord of the manor " had to measure the measures of the royal household, keep in order the female domestic servants, and dismember malefactors." A much lighter and pleasanter duty was that performed by Sir

William Russell. He held a manor in Dorsetshire for putting away the pieces after playing at
chess with the king.

Some tenures carry us back to the days when
ferocious animals roamed in the vast forests which
covered many parts of the country. Wolves
were general in England in bygone times. The
hunting of this animal was a popular pursuit of the
ancient Briton. The sport was attended with
considerable danger, and tales have come down
to us of huntsmen being devoured by the animals
they had delighted to follow. A story respecting
the wolf is linked with the discovery of the
medical properties of the mineral wells of Bath.
Far back into remote times, 863 years before the
birth of Christ, Blaiddyd occupied the throne of
Britain. He is credited with having some knowledge of chemistry, and he noticed that cattle,
after being wounded by wolves, went and stood
in the waters of the now famous wells of Bath,
whereupon the wounds quickly healed, and much
sooner than by any other treatment. Coming
down to times of which we have more certain
knowledge, we find it stated by several historians
that Edgar demanded, as an annual tribute from
the Welsh, the heads of three hundred wolves.

The tribute was paid for three years, but on the fourth year it ceased, as the animal had been totally destroyed. Says Somerville, in his poem " The Chase " :—

> " Cambria's proud kings (with reluctance) paid
>   Their tributary wolves ; head after head ;
>   In full account, till the woods yield no more,
>   And all the rav'nous race extinct is lost."

Commenting on this, Mr. J. E. Harting, in his " Extinct British Animals " (London, 1880), tells us that the statement refers only to Wales. He points out, " In the first place, it can hardly be supposed that the Welsh chieftain would be permitted to hunt out of his own dominions, and in the next place there is abundant documentary evidence to prove the existence of wolves in England for many centuries later." In the reign of Canute, Liuphus, dean of Whalley, was celebrated for hunting wolves in the forest of Rossendale. The " Lives of the Abbots of St. Albans," by Matthew Paris, contains a reference to the grant of church lands by Abbot Leofstan (the 12th abbott of the monastery) to Thurnoth and others, " on condition of their keeping the woods between the Chiltern Hundreds and London free from wolves and other wild animals."

William the Conqueror granted, in 1076, to
Robert de Umfraville the lordship of Riddesdale,
Northumberland, on condition that he defended
that part of the kingdom from his enemies and
wolves. In the reign of Henry III., Sir John de
Engayne held certain land at Pightesley, Northamptonshire, by the service of hunting the wolf
whenever the king should command him. William
de Limeres held, from the same king, a piece of
land, in Comelessend, by the service of hunting
the wolves with the king's dogs. Sir Robert
Plumpton held, so late as the eleventh year of the
reign of Henry VI., one bovate of land at Mans-
field Woodhouse, Nottinghamshire, called "Wolfhunt Land," by the service of winding a horn and
chasing or frightening the wolves in the forest of
Sherwood. In the adjoining county wolves
appear to have been troublesome. It may be
gathered from records in the Tower of London
that in 1320 lands were held at Wormhill by the
service of hunting and taking wolves. It is
asserted that a family called Wolfhunt, or Wolve-
hunt, derived their name from the services they
rendered.

Relating to the hunting of the wild-boar are
some interesting tenures. We gather from the

following translation of an old record that Edward III. hunted the wild-boar in Oxfordshire. "Anno 1339, 13th and 14th Edward III., an inquisition was taken on the death of Joan, widow of Thomas de Musgrove of Blechesdon, wherein it appears that said Joan held the moiety of one messuage and one carucate of land in Blechesdon of the king; by the service of carrying one boar-spear, price twopence, to the king, whenever he should hunt in the park of Cornbury; and do the same as often as the king should hunt, during his stay at his manor of Wodestock." Hunting the wild-boar was a favourite pastime of the townsmen of Grimsby, Lincolnshire. According to tradition, it was customary in the olden time, on the admission of a man to the freedom of the town, to present to the mayor a boar's head, or if the animal could not be procured, an equivalent in money. The manor of Bradley was held by tenure of keeping in the woods a supply of boars for an annual hunting match, which was officially proclaimed on some particular day after the Nativity of the Blessed Virgin. The sport was followed with spirit, and seldom did the day close without bringing down a leash of boars which provided important dishes for a feast held on the following day. At this feast the newly-elected mayor occupied a seat at the table; here were assembled the members of the Corporation, and leading gentlemen of the town and district. Before the mayor were placed two boars' heads, and before the marshal, one, and these constituted the chief fare for the festive gathering. The attachment of the members of the corporation to their ancient dish caused them to secure a provision for it in their agreement for letting the ferry between Grimsby and Hull for a certain period, commencing June 20th, 1620, at an annual rent of "one good and well-fed boar on the feast day of St. John Baptist, and one quarter of well-fed ox beef, and twenty shillings on the feast day of St. Thomas." Most probably the origin of the seal of the Corporation of Grimsby, a chevron between three boars' heads, is derived from the old-time custom of hunting the wild boar. At Hornchurch, Essex, formerly it was customary for the lessee of the tithes belonging to New College, Oxford, to supply a boar's head, dressed and garnished with bay leaves, to be wrestled for. It was carried in a procession to a field adjoining the churchyard, and there the competition was held. The rustic conqueror, after receiving the prize, usually feasted his friends on the boar's head.

Hawking or falconing was for several centuries a favourite sport. Many ancient tenures have provisions for providing birds for this pastime. It is recorded that in the year 1314, one Luke Barvill held a tenement at Barton-on-Humber, by paying into the royal exchequer of Edward II. a sparrow-hawk valued at two shillings. In the Harleian Manuscripts in the British Museum are several records relating to this theme and belonging to the county of Lincoln. In No. 34, p. 212, John de Clyxby, parson of the church of Symondesburne, Lincoln, admits he holds " one messuage and three oxgangs and a half of land, in Clyxby, of the Crown *in capite*, by the service of one hood and one falcon, to be paid to the King annually at Michaelmas, for all services ;" which said hood was apprised at a halfpenny. At the coronation of George IV., the Duke of Athol, as lord of the Isle of Man, presented his Majesty with two falcons. We gather from a report written at the time that these beautiful birds excited considerable curiosity. They sat perfectly tame on the arms of his grace, and were completely hooded and furnished with bells. In

1409, William de Molins held Aston, Bucks., by the service of finding the King's falcons, and presenting to his Majesty every year one sparrow-hawk. At Eton, in the same county, in bygone times, one Reginald de Grey held the manor by the service of rearing a falcon for the king, and, when ready for sport, taking it to court. In return he received the king's horse with its trappings, the table with trestle and tablecloth, all vessels used that day at the royal dinner, and a cask of wine immediately after the king had tasted it. We have drawn from Blount the preceding particulars. In his "Tenures of Land," many services relating to hawking are given, the lord of the manor of Eton appears to have been the most fortunate in receiving rewards for his trouble.

Thomas Astle, chief clerk of the records in the Tower, supplied to Beckwith, a writer on this subject, particulars of a tenure relating to fishing. It is one of a class of which numerous examples have come down to modern times. The details are as follows :—" Edward III. granted to Simon de Ringeley, and his heirs, a fish pond near Stafford, by the service of holding once the stirrup of the king, at the first mounting upon

his palfrey, every time of his coming to Stafford."
It appears from the Harleian collection that the
right of fishing was also granted to one Ralph
de Waymer. He held the privilege on condition
"that when the King should please to fish he was
to have the pikes and breams, and the said Ralph
and his heirs were to have all other fishes with
eels, coming to the hooks, rendering, therefor,
to the King half a mark at the Feast of St.
Michael." In Bloomfield's "History of Norwich"
are particulars of a curious custom connected with
the city of Norwich, which dates back to a time
when the valley of the Yare was still an estuary,
and when Yarmouth had not been founded. At
that period Norwich was an important fishing
station, though now it is some eighteen miles from
the sea. The particulars of the service may be
gathered from an old document. It reads as
follows :—

"This Indenture, made at Norwich, at the
Guildhall there, the twenty seventh of September,
at ten of ye clocke of ye forenoon of ye same day,
in ye twenty fifth year of ye reign of our Lord
Charles the 2nd, by ye grace of God of England,
Scotland, France, and Ireland, King, Defender of
ye Faith, &c., and in ye year of our Lord 1673,

BETWEEN John Leverington and Robert Freeman, sheriffs of ye city of Norwich, on one part, and Edward Eden, gentleman, tenant of Thomas Lurd Richardson, Baron of Cramond, &c., of ye other part, WITNESSETH, that ye aforesaid sheriffs, on ye day, houre, and place aforesaid, delivered to ye said Edward Eden, one hundred herrings (viz., of ye large hundred) of ye first new herrings that came to ye said city, in twenty four pies, well seasoned with ye following spices, viz., halfe a pounde of ginger, halfe a pounde of pepper, a quarter of cinnamon, one ounce of spice of cloves, one ounce of long pepper, halfe an ounce of grains of paradise, and halfe an ounce of galangals, to be brought to ye King's palace, wherever he is in England, and there to be delivered. AND be it known that ye said Edward Eden or his attorney carrying ye said pyes, shall receive at the king's house six loves, six dishes out of ye kitchen, one flaggon of wine, one flaggon of beer, one truss of hay, one bushel of oats, one prickett of wax, and six candles of tallow ; IN TESTIMONY of whiche ye parties aforesaid have alternately set their seals to this Indenture, ye day, houre, and place, and yeare aforesaid."

Blomefield reproduces a letter dated iiij Oct. 1629, from the officers of the royal household, addressed to the mayor and sheriffs of the city, in which it was asserted that the pies "were not well-baked in good and strong payste as they ought to have been." "Divers of them," it is further stated, "also, were found to contain no more than four herrings, whereas the tenure required five to be put in every pye at least." It was also said that they were not made from the first new herrings which had reached the city. Other exceptions were taken to their goodness, and his Majesty demanded better satisfaction. The cost of the pies is put down at two pounds, but this does not include carriage.

We found in the columns of *Aris's Birmingham Gazette*, of June 22nd, 1789, the following particulars of a curious custom, and a record of its observance :—" Sir Charles Mills, an elderly clergyman," it is stated, "holds a Royalty of his Majesty, the Manor of Langley, on condition of presenting his Majesty, whenever he passes that way, with a brace of white greyhounds, with silver collars, coupled together with a gold chain, and led with a silken string. This ceremony was performed on his Majesty coming to his home in the

Forest." Several grants of land were made for attending to the dogs of the King. One person held land for keeping for his Majesty a white bitch with red ears; another was rewarded with an estate for taking care of the lame dogs of the king.

According to Camden's "Britannica," "Bradford belonged to John of Gaunt, who granted to John Northorp, of Manningham, and his heirs, three messuages and six bovates of land, to come to Bradford on the blowing of a horn in winter, and to wait upon him and his heirs on their way from Blackburnshire, with a lance and hunting dog for thirty days; to have for yeoman's bond one penny for himself and one halfpenny for his dog. A descendant of this Northorp afterwards granted land to Rushworth of Horton, to hold the lance while Northorp's man blew the horn. The name of Hornblowing Land was imposed upon the lands in question." In the olden time horns played an important part in tenures and manorial customs, as we have shewn in our recently published volume, "Old Church Lore."

For a long period a curious custom was observed at St. Paul's Cathedral, London. Its origin dates back to the year 1375, when Sir

William Bard was allowed to enclose twenty acres
of land belonging to the church on condition of
presenting annually to the clergy a fat buck and
doe, upon the days of the Conversion and
Commemoration of St. Paul. The animals were
carried with ceremony to the high altar, where
the dean and chapter, attired in their copes and
proper vestments, and decorated with garlands
of roses, awaited their arrival. It is recorded
that "the buck's body was sent to be baked; but
the head and horns being fixed upon a pole, were
carried before the cross, round about the church.
On reaching the west door the keeper 'blowed
the death of the buck,' and was answered by
sundry horns about the city." The blowers were
provided with their dinner and three and four pence
each; the keeper received five shillings, and a
loaf of bread stamped with St. Paul's image, and
those who brought the buck were presented with
twelve pence.

A few military tenures must next receive our
consideration. A knight at Harkercet, County
Salop, held the manor by the service of sending
one archer with a bow and three arrows, when the
king went to Wales, in the time of war. His
duty was done when he had discharged the arrows

F

at the enemy. In the same county, we gather from Blount that Robert Cortet held the manor of Chettington by the service of finding one footman in the time of war, in the king's army in Wales. He had to be provided with one bow, three arrows, and one pale, and one bacon or salted hog. On entering the army, he had to deliver to the marshal the bacon, and he received daily from him a portion of it for his dinner, and remained as long as it lasted. It has been suggested that if the marshal required the services of the man for a long period, a scanty dinner would be given, but if he was not likely to be needed, a bountiful repast would be cut.

There are instances of manors being held on condition of saying prayers. The repeating of a Paternoster daily for the king's soul was the service rendered for holding a manor. The lord of the manor of Apse, in Surrey, held certain land on condition of giving away a cask of ale upon All Saints' Day, for the soul of the king and his ancestors.

There are many well-authenticated instances of floral services, not the least curious being the rendering of a snow ball in summer, and a rose at Christmas. At Bermony, Perthshire, James V.

granted lands to the Haldane family. It is said
that the king paid a visit to the place in disguise,
and was kindly entertained by "the guidwife,"
and as a mark of his gratitude he granted lands
on the conditions named in the following
rhyme :—

> "Ye Haddens o' the Moor, ye pay nocht
> But a harren tether, if its socht,
> And red rose at Yule, and a sna' ba' at Lammas."

Many and curious are the tenures and customs
connected with Christmastide, and with the
consideration of a few linked with the season we
must close our chapter. In the days of King
John, the Lord Percys came into the possession
of the manor of Leconfield, East Yorkshire, on
condition that they proceeded every Christmas-
day to Skelton Castle, escorted the lady of that
stronghold to chapel to attend mass, and then
returned and dined with her. The Countess of
Warwick held Hoke Norton by the service of
carving the king's Christmas dinner. She was
allowed to carry away the carving-knife. We
gather from the Harleian manuscripts that the
manor of Hawarden was formerly "held of the
king *in capite* by Robert de Montrault, Earl of
Arundel, by being Steward of the County of

Chester, viz. :—by the service of setting down the first dish before the Earl of Chester, at Chester, on Christmas-day." At North Clifton, Nottinghamshire, the inhabitants were entitled to cross the ferry free of charge. In return for this, the ferryman and his dog were entertained with dinner at the vicarage at Christmas, and at the same time the villagers gave him a loaf of bread. The parishioners of Cumnor, Berkshire, who paid vicarial tithes claimed on the afternoon of Christmas-day, bread, cheese, and beer. Prior to that day, four bushels of malt were brewed into ale, two bushels of wheat were made into bread, and half a hundredweight of cheese was provided. After divine service the next day, the poor of the place received the food and drink which was left. Shaw, the historian of Staffordshire, relates in his work, that in bygone time it was customary for the rector of Great Barr, on Christmas, to give to all persons coming to his house as much bread, beef, mustard, and vinegar as they could eat. At Wadsley Hall, a strange custom was observed in the olden time. It was the practice for the lord or owner of Wadsley Hall to maintain twelve men and their horses "at free commons twelve days in Christmas, and when they went away, every one stuck a large pin or a needle in the mantle tree." The Greens, of Green Norton, held their manor by the service of lifting up the right hand towards the king upon Christmas-day. A curious custom was enacted by Rowland le Sarcere, of Hemington, Suffolk. The ceremony is described in an old deed as follows :—" On Christmas-day, every year, before our Sovereign Lord the King of England, he should perform altogether, and at once, a leap and a puff." Blount explains the performance by saying that " he should dance and puff up his cheeks, making therewith a sound." We find it stated in Hutchins' " History of Dorsetshire," that the family of Erles held the manor of Parva Somerton, or Somerton Erleigh, by the service of pouring water on the king's hands at Easter, or at Christmas.

Curiosities of Slavery in England.

SLAVERY existed in England for a long period. It existed when Cæsar landed here. During the whole of the Anglo-Saxon times slaves were sold like cattle in the open market. They consisted of slaves by right of conquest; of others sold into slavery by their parents, or by their own free will; thieves found guilty of stealing were often sold as slaves as a punishment of their crimes; not a few were doomed to slavery through not being able to pay penalties imposed for breaking the laws of the land; and lastly, we find traces of men voluntarily surrendering their liberty for food. Famines at this time occurred very often, and men were glad to be slaves for their daily bread. A parent might sell his child if it had reached the age of seven years, and at thirteen the child might sell itself into slavery. A slave was generally estimated at four times the value of an ox. In the reign of King Athelstan the punishment for theft was most severe, and on the authority of Lingard we state that "a law was made respecting the offences committed by slaves against others than their masters. A man thief was ordered to be stoned to death by twenty of his fellows, each of whom was punished with three whippings, if he failed thrice to hit the culprit. A woman thief was burnt by eighty women slaves, each of whom brought three billets of wood to the execution. If she failed, she was likewise subjected to the punishment of three whippings. After the death of the offender, each slave paid three pennies as a fine to the proprietor."

As Christianity spread, the condition of the slave became happier than before its truths were known. The slave might still be sold at the pleasure of the owner, but with the restriction that a Christian was not to be made over to a Pagan.

It appears the freeing of a slave was attended with some ceremony. It was enacted in public— in the market-place, in the court of the hundred, or in the church, at the foot of the principal altar. The owner of the slave took his hand, offered it to the bailiff, sheriff, or clergyman, and handing to the freedman a sword and a lance, intimated to him that the ways and gates were open, and that he was at liberty to go wheresoever he felt disposed.

Many slaves were exported to Ireland and Scotland by the Anglo-Saxons, but as soon as William the Conqueror ruled the country, he sternly repressed the practice. Bristol was the last town in England to hold a slave-market. Wulfustan, Bishop of Worcester, who died in 1095, did much to repress it by his powerful preaching against the barbarity and irreligion of dealing in slaves.

"At last," it is stated, "the merchants were convinced by his reasons, and in their gild solemnly bound themselves to renounce the trade. One of the members was soon afterwards tempted to violate his engagement. His perfidy was punished by the loss of his eyes." At the time of the Domesday Survey, the toll in the market-place of Lewes, in Sussex, was one penny for the sale of an ox, and fourpence for that of a slave.

No sooner had Edward VI. ascended the throne than the following statute was made :—" That a runaway, or any one who lived idly for three days, should be brought before two justices of the peace, and marked V with a hot iron on the breast, and adjudged the slave of him who brought him for two years. He was to take the slave and give him bread, water, or small drink, and refuse meat, and cause him to work by beating, chaining, or otherwise ; and if within that space he absented himself fourteen days, he was to be marked on the forehead or cheek, by a hot iron, with an S, and be his master's slave for ever ; a second desertion was made felony. It was lawful to put a ring of iron round his neck, arm, or leg. A child might be put apprentice, and running away, become a slave to his master." Coming still further down the stream of time until we are at the year of grace 1660, we then reach the period of the downfall of the slavery of English-born people in their native land, for serfdom ended for ever in this country.

Although we have reached the time when Englishmen were no longer slaves on their native soil, we get glimpses through the newspapers of negroes still being sold in this country. If we turn over the advertising columns of the old newspapers, we discover advertisements similar to the following, copied from the *London Gazette*, of 1688 : " Run away from his master, Captain St. Lo, the 21st, instant, Obdelah Elalias Abraham, a Moor, swarthy complexion, short frizzled hair, a gold ring in his ear, in a black coat and breeches. He took with him a blue Turkish watch-gown, a Turkish suit of clothing that he used to wear about town, and several other things. Whoever brings him to Mr. Lozel's house in Green Street shall have a guinea for his charges." Here is another notice of a runaway slave, extracted from the same journal for 1694. "A black boy, an Indian, about thirteen years old, ran away the 8th instant from Putney, with a collar about his neck, with this inscription : 'The Lady Bromfield's black in Lincoln's Inn Fields.' Whoever brings him to Sir Edward Bromfield's at Putney shall have a guinea reward." It may be inferred, from the frequency of advertisements like the foregoing, that slaves very often ran away from their owners. We find in the *Tatler*, of 1709, the following : "A black boy, twelve years of age, fit to wait on a gentleman, to be disposed of at Dennis's Coffee-house in Finch Lane, near the Royal Exchange." In the *Daily Journal*, of September 28th, 1728, there appears : "To be sold, a negro boy, aged eleven years. Enquire of the Virginia Coffee-house, Threadneedle Street, behind the Royal Exchange."

The following, extracted from *Aris's Birmingham Gazette*, 1771, is perhaps the last advertisement of a slave for sale in England :—

"November 11, 1771. To be Sold by Auction, on Saturday the 30th day of November, instant. at the House of Mrs. Webb, in the City of Lichfield, and known by the Sign of the Baker's Arms, between the Hours of Three and Five in the Evening of the same day, and subject to Articles that will be then and there produced (except sold by private Contract before the Time, of which Notice will be given to the Public) by John Heeley, of Walsall, Auctioneer and Salesman, A Negro Boy from Africa, supposed to be about Ten or Eleven Years of Age. He is remarkably strait, well-proportioned, speaks tolerably good English, of a mild Disposition, friendly, officious, sound, healthy, fond of Labour, and for Colour an excellent fine Black. For particulars enquire of the said John Heeley."

A year after the foregoing advertisement appeared, namely, in 1772, a slave named Somerset was brought to England, but on account of ill-health, was cast adrift by his master ; happily the poor fellow came under the notice of Mr. Granville Sharp, who restored him to health. His master again claimed him, but after a trial at the Court of King's Bench, it was decided that slavery could not exist in Great Britain.

Buying and Selling in the Olden Time.

THE regulations respecting buying and selling in the olden days were very strict. In Hull, for example, in and prior to the year 1452, it was customary for the mayor and sheriff to proclaim in the Market Place certain bye-laws and ordinances, and to take care that they were properly observed. After directing : " That all the king's liege people keep his majesty's peace, and that no burgess or inhabitant draw any knife, sword, or any other offensive weapon, in breach of the same, under a penalty of 3s. and 4d.," it was directed : " That no man purchase any victuals coming to the market before they be got thither, under a penalty of 3s. and 4d." Says the next bye-law : " That no person dwelling within the town buy any fish, flesh, or wild fowl, to sell again to another inhabitant, under penalty of forfeiting the same, imprisonment of body, and fine to the king." The Hull people were compelled to trade with their own bakers, for a local law directed that no one sell or buy bread in the town, but what is made or baked therein.

Our forefathers were not only particular as to the time and place of selling goods, but were careful that their quality was satisfactory. According to the Liverpool town records, in the year 1558, the mayor of Liverpool received instructions to have a proclamation made at the cross, that "no shoemaker of the countrie doe bring shoes to sell in Liverpole market made of horse hyde or of unlawful barked leather." If the vendor broke this law three times, he was banished from the market.

We find in the Court Leet records of Manchester, that in 1591, no person was permitted to buy on any other than the market day, and in no other place except the open market. The inhabitants had the privilege of making their purchases between nine and ten o'clock, and after that time strangers were allowed to buy in the market. If the law was broken, and the fact became known, half the fruit was taken by the lord of the manor, and the other half went to the officers of the court. Six years later, namely in 1597, the Court Leet jury resolved that no foreigner, nor any other stranger, shall sell or measure any corn upon any other day than the Saturday and Monday, and that to be after the

bell rings. The same records for 1595, contain a
regulation on this subject, stating that "No man
shall sell any corn in any house upon the market
day, and neither open any sack, nor make any
price of the said corn and grain, until the market
bell be rung."

At Preston, Lancashire, the inhabitants enjoyed
the privilege of purchasing goods in the market
from eight till nine o'clock on market day morn-
ings, strangers and hucksters not being permitted
to buy any goods during the time. From nine till
one o'clock the market was open to anybody. At
one p.m. the market was closed, and before that
time nothing except fish could be withdrawn
unsold.

A paragraph in the *Preston Review* for July
13th, 1793, bears on this subject. It is stated
that "On Saturday last, Thomas Cross, of
Shaw Hill, Esq., was convicted before the Worshipful the Mayor of this Borough in the sum of
ten shillings for buying poultry within one of the
markets of this town before the usual hour of the
inhabitants having a right to purchase the same,
which his Worship was pleased to mitigate to six
shillings and eightpence, and which was paid
accordingly. At the same time a woman, the

vendor of the above-mentioned poultry, was convicted in, and paid, the like penalty."

The business of the town of Barton-on-
Humber, Lincolnshire, in the olden days, was
conducted under certain bye-laws which appear in
a book dated 1670, and which were copied from a
book in existence in 1600. Mr. H. W. Ball, the
local historian, reproduces some items from the
old regulations. "To prevent coals being dear,"
says Mr. Ball, "the town authorities took the
price out of the dealers' hands, and enacted that
the master of every vessel entering the haven
with coals should not sell them either to a 'Barton man' or to any 'countryman' until the fore-
man of the jury had fixed the saleable value, and
received half a well of coals for his trouble.
Dissentient captains were peremptorily ordered
out of the haven, and fined ten shillings for every
day's delay in quitting it." We are also told that
"there was a law prohibiting any person purchasing for resale at a profit any goods brought into
the haven, until after the expiration of three days
from the bellman's announcing the arrival of the
cargo. During these three days, the inhabitants
had the opportunity of buying the goods at the
wholesale price."

The law relating to forestalling or engrossing may be traced back to the days of Edward III. In 1350 a statute was passed rendering anyone buying articles of food on the way to a market liable to forfeit the things bought, or two years' imprisonment.

Several Acts were subsequently passed for its suppression, the repeal being finally made as late as July 24th, 1844.

Curious Fair Customs.

OLD fair customs are numerous and curious, and form an interesting feature in the annals of trade. A study of a few of the more important usages can hardly fail to be of interest and value in throwing side lights on life in the olden time, and more especially that relating to commercial activity.

The hoisting of a large glove in several old English towns was, from time immemorial, a signal for commencing the fairs. Amongst the many towns where this custom obtained may be mentioned Barnstaple, Exeter, Portsmouth, Southampton, Macclesfield, Liverpool, and Chester. The opening of the Lammas Fair at Exeter was attended with some little ceremony, in which the glove was a conspicuous object. A procession started from Westgate consisting of the head-constable, bearing a roll of parchment tied with blue ribbons containing the charter granted for holding the fair ; two staff bearers wearing three-cornered hats ; a couple of fifers and a drummer were also present playing, and these were followed by a man carrying a long blue and white pole, decorated with flowers, and surmounted with a large white glove stuffed. It is almost superfluous to add that an immense number of children assisted in the procession. A halt was made at the old gates of the city, and the charter read by the head-constable. After the perambulation, the glove was mounted in front of the Guildhall, and remained there three days, being the time the fair lasted. At Barnstaple the pole bearing the glove was decked with dahlias, and exhibited during the fair in front of Quay Hall, the most ancient building in the town. In addition to exhibiting the glove in front of the Liverpool Town Hall, some curious customs were observed. It was the practice in the olden time for the burgesses with arms to attend the mayor when he opened the fair. We gather from the Liverpool records, under the date of 27th October, 1589, that it was agreed:—"That all free burgesses beinge within the Town shall give theire attendance and wait upon Mr. Maior with a halberde or bill, or other convenient weapon, to be carried by him or his servante upon two faire days in his perambulations, etc., upon paine

of xijd. for every defaulte." Formerly boundary
stones marked the privileged precincts of the fair,
and for ten days before and after the fair anyone
visiting it for lawful business could not legally be
arrested within the area indicated by the stones.
" This," says Sir J. A. Picton, in his " Memorials
of Liverpool," " may seem a trifle now, but in the
days when any man might be summarily arrested
and thrown into gaol on the merest pretence of a
debt, it was a wholesome provision." The custom
of hoisting the glove at the fair continued at
Liverpool until the period of the Municipal
Reform Act. A large boundary stone remained
in Castle Street until recent years, when it was
removed to make way for the tramway.

Several attempts have been made to trace the
origin of this custom. One writer says the glove
was selected at Chester as a sign of the fair on
account of being the principal article offered for
sale. This cannot by any means be regarded as
a satisfactory solution, as the practice prevailed
where gloves were not the staple commodity.
A note in " *Speculum Saxonicum* " bearing on
this subject is of considerable interest. " No
one," says the writer, " is allowed to set up a
market or a mint, without the consent of the

ordinary or judge of that place, the king also ought to send a glove as a sign of his consent to the same." We may, we think, safely infer from the foregoing that the glove represents the king's glove, and the earliest form of the royal charter, the "sign manual."

The fair at Portsmouth used to last fifteen days. On the 9th of July, at midnight, the town-sergeant "put out the glove" at the Town Hall. It consisted of an open hand in a gauntlet. We gather from a note written by Mr. W. H. Long, that in the year 1840, the hand was stolen and forwarded to America. He says the purloiner imagined its absence would put an end to holding the fair. Three years later the townsmen purchased by subscription another open hand. It is described as being "of natural size, naked, the wrist in gilded mail, and on the fore-finger a ring bearing the device of Richard I., a crescent and seven-rayed star, being also the arms of the borough granted by the king." The fair was discontinued in 1846, and with it ended a custom which had long been popular in Portsmouth.

The October fair at Croydon was formerly opened at midnight after the sounding of the town clock, or in earlier times of the parish

clock, by the carrying through the principal
avenue of the fair a large key known as " the key
of the fair." After the bearer of the key had
perambulated the place, the booth-keepers were
at liberty to commence selling refreshments.
Long before daylight the business of the fair was
in active operation.

In bygone times it was a common custom to
ring church bells before the fairs commenced.
Formerly one of the bells of St. Nicholas' Church,
Newcastle-on-Tyne, was rung as a signal for
suspicious characters, including thieves, to enter
the town with perfect freedom, and remain during
the fair without fear of being imprisoned for
crimes previously committed.

Some singular customs prevailed at York in
bygone times in connection with the Lammas
Fair.   The day before Old Lammas Day, at
three o'clock in the afternoon, a bell at St.
Michael's Church was rung, and on hearing it,
the sheriffs of the city gave up their authority
during the fair to the representatives of the Archbishop of York.   They handed over their white
rods of office, and had not the power of arresting
persons in the city and suburbs during the fair.
The Archbishop's officials had the control of the

city during the fair, and stationed men at the
gates of the city to collect tolls for animals and
wares coming in and out of York. A Piepowder
Court was held for trying offences committed at
the fair, and the members of the jury selected for
hearing the cases were chosen from men out of
Wistow, a township situated within the Archbishop's liberty. At three p.m. the day following
Old Lammas Day, the fair was closed, and the
ringing of a church bell was the intimation of the
time for the sheriffs to receive back their white
wands, and to resume their duties. The Lammas
Fair was not the only occasion that questionable
men and women might with safety repair to York.
During the twelve days of Christmastide, the
sheriffs, after attending mass, proceeded to the
Pillory in the Pavement, and after the blowing of
horns, declared that all "manner of thieves, dice-
players, and all other unthrifty folk, be welcomed
to the town, whether they come late or early, at
the reverence of the high feast of Yule till the
twelve days be passed." In some places the ringing customs are still in force. At Epworth,
Lincolnshire, for example, a merry peal is rung
the night before the annual fair.

Drake, in his *Eboracum*, refers to a fair that was

annually held at York on St. Luke's Day for the sale of small-wares, and known as Dish-fair, from the quantity of wooden dishes, ladles, etc., offered for sale. Connected with this fair was an old custom of bearing a wooden ladle in a sling, carried by four sturdy labourers ; this being, no doubt, in ridicule of the meanness of the wares brought to the fair.

St. Luke's Day was formerly known in York as Whip-dog Day, from the strange custom of boys whipping all dogs found in the streets on this day.

As to the origin of the persecution, several suggestions have been made. Some writers have thought it comes down from Roman times. Drake regards the following tradition as most probable : —" That in some time of popery, a priest, celebrating mass at this festival in some church in York, unfortunately dropped the host after consecration, which was suddenly snatched up and swallowed by a dog that lay under the altar table. The profanation of this high mystery occasioned the death of the dog, and a persecution began, which was continued on the anniversary of this day."

Whipping dogs at fairs was not confined to York, as we have traces of it at Rotherham,

Sheffield, Hull, and other places.   Mr. John
Richardson, a well-known collector of local lore,
contributed to *Notes and Queries* an interesting
account of the custom.   " There was," says Mr.
Richardson, "sometime since the singular custom
in Hull of whipping all the dogs that were found
running about the streets on October 10th, and
some thirty years since, when I was a boy, so
common was the practice, that every little urchin
considered it his duty to prepare a whip for any
unlucky dog that might be seen in the streets on
this day.   This custom is now obsolete, those
'putters down' of all boys' play in the streets—
the new police—having effectually stopped the
cruel practice of the Hull boys.   Perhaps some of
your readers may be able to give a more correct
origin of this singular custom than the one I
now render from tradition : 'Previous to the
suppression of monasteries in Hull, it was the
custom for the monks to provide liberally for the
poor and wayfarers who came to the fair held
annually on the 11th October ; and while busy in
the necessary preparation, the day before the fair,
a dog strolled into the larder, snatched up a joint
of meat, and decamped with it.   The cooks gave
alarm ; and when the dog got into the street he

was pursued by the expectants of the charity of
the monks, who were waiting outside the gates,
and made to give up the stolen joint. Whenever
after this a dog showed his face while the annual
preparation was going on, he was instantly beaten
off. Eventually this was taken up by the boys,
and, until the introduction of the new police, was
rigidly put in practice by them every 10th
October.' I write on the 10th October, 1853,
and so effectually has this custom been suppressed,
that I have neither seen nor heard of any dog
whipped according to ancient custom."

Hunter, the historian of Hallamshire, describes
dog-whipping in 1802, at Sheffield and Rotherham. Writing in 1821, he says the barbarous
practice of dog-whipping has been discontinued
in his district.

The custom of walking the fair was performed
in many places. Mr. Charles Henry Poole
presents particulars of several of these ceremonies
enacted in Staffordshire in his "Customs of the
County of Stafford." "At Wolverhampton,"
says Mr. Poole, "on the 9th of July, the eve of
the great fair, there was formerly a procession of
men in antique armour, preceded by musicians
playing the fair tune, and followed by the steward

of the Deanery Manor, the peace officers, and
many of the principal inhabitants. Tradition
affirms that the ceremony originated when the
town was a great emporium for wool, and resorted
to by merchants of the staple, from all parts of
England. The necessity of an armed force to
keep peace during the fair, which is said to have
lasted fourteen days, is not improbable." It is
suggested by one authority that the procession is
the remains of the Corpus Christi pageantry. The
practice of walking the fair was discontinued
about 1789.

It is about one thousand years ago since Alfred
the Great instituted fairs in England. They
were popular amongst the Saxons, and our first
Norman king recognised their value as a means
of extending commerce. He framed Acts for the
better conducting of trade, etc. One of the
greatest of our mediæval time fairs was established
by William the Conqueror at Winchester, on St.
Giles's Down. The story of its rise and fall does
not come within the scope of this chapter. We
must content ourselves with reproducing from
Brand's "Popular Antiquities" a few particulars
respecting its history. "Its jurisdiction," says
Brand, "extends seven miles round, and

comprehends even Southampton, then a capital
and a trading town. Merchants who sold wares
at that time within that circuit forfeited them to
the bishop. Officers were placed at a considerable distance, at bridges and other avenues of
access to the fair, to exact toll of all merchandise
passing that way. In the meantime, all shops in
the city of Winchester were shut. A court called
the Pavilion, composed of the bishop's justiciaries
and other officers, had power to try causes of
various sorts for seven miles round. The bishop
had a toll of every load or parcel of goods passing
through the gates of the City. On St. Giles's
Eve, the mayor, bailiffs, and citizens of
Winchester, delivered the keys of the four gates
to the bishop's officers. Many and extraordinary
were the privileges granted to the bishop on this
occasion, all tending to obstruct trade, and to
oppress the people. Numerous foreign
merchants attended this fair; and several streets
were formed in it, assigned to the sale of different
commodities. The surrounding monasteries had
shops or houses in the streets, used only at the
fair, which they held under the bishop, and often
let by lease for a term of years. Different
counties had their different stations."

When this fair was first established it only lasted for three days. It was subsequently prolonged to sixteen days by Henry III. Brand says that William I. gave the tolls of this fair as a kind of revenue to the Bishop of Winchester.

No fair in England was more celebrated than that of Stourbridge. An excellent account of it may be found in the pages of "Fairs Past and Present," by Cornelius Walford. He tells us that the first trace of it is found in a charter granted about 1211 by King John to the Lepers of the Hospital of St. Mary Magdalen, at Stourbridge, by Cambridge — a fair to be held in the close of the Hospital on the Vigil and Feast of the Holy Cross. Its history shows how subsequently contentions arose between the town and University of Cambridge, in respect to the profits and control of this fair. It was held on a large piece of land near the banks of the Cam. It has been stated that John Bunyan viewed this fair, and that it suggested to him the idea of Vanity Fair. We learn from the records of this fair that in 1655 a crimson coat, gaily decorated with taps, was bought for the Lord of Taps, whose duty it was to taste the ale in any or all the booths of the fair, and see if they were fit for consumption.

Defoe visited this fair in 1723, and in the following year published an account of it. Referring to the field where the fair was held, he states that "if the husbandmen who rent the land do not get their corn off before a certain day in August, the fair-keepers may trample it under feet and spoil it to build their booths. On the other hand, to balance that severity, if the fair-keepers have not done their business of the fair, and removed and cleared the field by another certain day in September, the ploughmen may come in again, with plough and cart, and overthrow all, and trample it into the dirt." The fair used to be proclaimed with much ceremony, and in 1855 the authorities of the University proclaimed it for the last time.

We bring this chapter to a close with some notes drawn from a Manchester newspaper of 24th October, 1891, relating to a relic of feudalism lingering at Dalton-in-Furness. It is recorded that on the 24th of October annually a document as follows is read at the cross in presence of a few javelin men:—"Thomas Woodburn, steward unto the most noble the Duke of Buccleuch and Queensberry, lord of the late dissolved monastery and manor of Furness, and liberty of the same, strictly chargeth and commandeth all manner of persons repairing to the fair, of what estate or degree soever he or they be, that they and every of them keep the Queen's Majesty's peace, every knight upon pain of £10, every squire and gentleman upon pain of £5, and every other person upon pain of 40s. And that no person or persons have or bear any habiliments of war, steel coats, bills or battle axes, but such as are appointed to attend upon the said steward during this present fair. And that none do buy or sell any wares, but by such yards and wands as are or shall be delivered unto them by the bailiff of the town of Dalton. And the fair to last three days, whereof this is the second, and if any wrong be done or offered to any person or persons, he or they may repair to the said steward to have justice ministered unto them according to law. God save the Queen and the lord of this fair."

It is further reported that subsequently a meeting is held at the Castle, and juries are appointed for various purposes, and from amongst these two gentlemen are selected as " ale-tasters." These ale-tasters are bound to visit all the public houses in Dalton and taste the ale, their omission of any house being met with a fine. They make a report, and those having the best ale are awarded a " red ribbon," the second best obtaining a " blue ribbon." As the fair is being held just now, red and blue ribbon ales are in demand. It is said that this custom dates from the time when the Abbot of Furness was supplied with ale from Dalton, and this was regularly tasted by specially appointed ale-tasters to avoid the chance of my lord the Abbot being poisoned.

Old Prejudices Against Coal.

THE history of coal reads like a romance, and presents facts of a curious and interesting character. It is generally believed that the ancient Britons burned coal before the arrival of the Romans in this country. Our Anglo-Saxon ancestors consumed it to a limited extent, but, remarkable to relate, it is not named in the annals of the Danish usurpation nor under the Norman monarchs.

Perhaps the earliest document in which coal is mentioned is in " Bishop Pudsey's Boldon Book," and it is in the year 1183. It is generally asserted that in the year 1234, Henry III. granted a charter to the freemen of Newcastle-on-Tyne "to dig stones and coal" in the common soil without the walls of the town. But it is proved beyond doubt, after recent and careful investigation, that this statement must be regarded as an historical fiction. It was not until the reign of Edward III., and in the year 1350, that the townsmen of Newcastle received such a privilege.

Between 1260-63, Walter de Clifford obtained permission from the king "to dig coals within the forests of Le Clie, to sell or give away." This was the earliest notice of coal in Shropshire. Coal-pits are named at Wednesbury in 1315. Much of the coal at this early period was most probably quarried, and not mined. The Earl of Winchester, some time between the years 1210 and 1219, granted to the monks of Newbattle, Midlothian, a coalfield situated between the burn of Whytrig and the lands of Pontekyn, Inveresk. This is understood to be the first coal worked in Scotland. The monks of Dunfermline soon followed the example of their brethren at Newbattle, and obtained coal from lands in their possession. For nearly a century after the discovery of the "blackstone," as it was called, the peasantry were its chief consumers.

In the reign of Edward I., the aversion to this fuel was most pronounced, and a proclamation was issued prohibiting its use in London. Even dyers, brewers, etc., were forbidden to burn coal on pain of a fine, loss of furnace, etc. This stringent law was not merely confined to the city ; it extended to the suburbs. The proclamation was brought about by the prelates, nobles, and gentry, who complained that they could not stay in town on account of "the noisome smell and thick air" caused by burning coal. Stow, referring to this period, says :—" The nice dames of London would not come into any house or room where sea-coals were burned, nor willingly eat of the meat that was even sod or roasted with sea-coal." It was in the reign of Edward I. that a man was tried, convicted, and executed for the crime of burning sea-coal in London. The students of Oxford and Cambridge were not permitted to have fires until the days of Henry VIII., and to warm themselves they ran for some distance—certainly a cheap mode of obtaining warmth.

Towards the reign of Elizabeth, coal was becoming a popular kind of fuel, chiefly owing to the difficulty of obtaining a cheap and plentiful supply of wood. A strong prejudice, however, lingered against it, and the queen prohibited the burning of coal in London during the sitting of Parliament, for it was feared that "the health of the knights of the shires might suffer during their abode in the metropolis." In the days of Charles I., the use of coal became very general, and as the demand increased, the price went up to such

an extent as to preclude the poor from obtaining
it. Not a few died from cold for want of fires.
In 1643 was published a pamphlet, stating on the
imprint :—

> " Printed in the year
> That sea-coal was exceeding dear."

Duties were laid on coal after the Great Fire of
London to raise money to rebuild St. Paul's and
fifty other churches. Charles II., in the year
1677, granted to one of his natural children and
his heirs a duty on coal of one shilling per
chaldron. This tax was known as the " Richmond Shilling," and was continued down to 1800,
when it was purchased by the Government.

The last of London coal dues ended on July 5th
1890. "Almost without notice in the north of
England," said a Newcastle-on-Tyne newspaper,
"the tax upon one of its industries has been brought
to an end. We refer to the London coal duty,
which, after existing from time immemorial, ceased
on Saturday last. The duty has varied in amount
at different times, but from 1807 to 1889, it
amounted to thirteenpence per ton, levied on all coal
brought into the area of the City or the Metro-
politan police district. It was to have expired on
July 5 last year, but a portion of the entire duty,

amounting to fourpence per ton, was allowed by
Parliament to be levied for another year, in order
to aid in meeting with the deficiency connected
with the Holborn valley improvements. In 1886
the complete duty of thirteenpence produced
£450,000, equivalent to a rate of nearly fourpence
in the pound. If still existing the duty would yield
a yet higher amount, as the fourpence per ton for the
half-year ending last December would have produced £77,000. Accordingly, it may be reckoned
that a duty of thirteenpence per ton would now produce half a million sterling in relief of the rates."

Charles, also, in 1662, imposed a tax known as
the "hearth-tax." on every fireplace or hearth in
England, and he raised by it about £200,000 per
annum. It was abolished by William and Mary
after the revolution in 1689, imposed again, and
subsequently abolished. A quaint epitaph at
Folkestone to the memory of Rebecca Rodgers,
who died on August 22nd, 1688, aged 44 years,
refers to the tax as follows : —

> " A home she hath : it's made of such good fashion
> The tenant ne'er shall pay for reparation ;
> Nor will her landlord ever raise the rent,
> Or turn her out of doors for non-payment ;
> From chimney money, too, this cell is free :
> To such a house who would not tenant be ? "

The Sedan Chair.

THE Sedan Chair is named after Sedan, the town where it was first used. The earliest mention of it in England occurs in 1581. Early in the following century the Duke of Buckingham caused much indignation by its use in London. People were exasperated at that nobleman employing his fellowmen to take the place of horses to carry him. Prince Charles brought from Spain, in 1623, three curiously-wrought sedans, two of which he gave to the Duke of Buckingham. A few weeks after their introduction, Massinger produced his play the *Bondman*, and in it he thus adverts to the ladies :—

> " For their pomp and care being borne
> In triumph *on men's shoulders.*"

The reference is doubtless to Buckingham's sedan which was borne like a palanquin.

A letter written on the 8th February, 1645, by John Evelyn, from Naples, gives an account of the gay appearance of the city and its people. " The streets," says Evelyn, " are full of gallants on

horseback, in coaches and sedans." He goes on
to say that from hence the sedan chair was
brought first into England by Sir Sanders
Duncomb. He, in 1634, obtained a patent
granting him for fourteen years the sole privilege
of using and letting sedan chairs in England. It
was stated in this patent that " the lives and limbs
of his majesty's subjects were greatly endangered
by the multitude of coaches in London and Westminster, and that the chairs would be a proper
substitute." In appearance these chairs were like
the body of a brougham of our time. They were not
large, and were usually constructed to carry one
inside. On each side were two square staples,
through which poles were passed, and thus shafts
were formed before and behind, by this means
the passenger being carried by two men. This
mode of conveyance soon became popular, and
continued in favour for about two hundred
years.

Duncomb was a physician, and it is suggested
that he recommended the use of the chair in this
country in the first instance in the interests of
invalids. In Manchester one was used for the
sick in the first half of this century. Mrs. Geo.
Linnæus Banks, the author of " The Manchester

Man," and other popular novels, furnishes us with an interesting note on this subject. " Prior to 1830," says Mrs. Banks, "there was a sedan chair kept in the vestibule of the Manchester Infirmary. It was straight up and down, was covered with black leather secured to the wooden frame with rows of brass-headed nails. Its windows were curtained, and it was borne on poles by two men, at the downward stretch of their arms." The chair, we are told, was only used at long intervals, and for carrying sick to the infirmary. Mrs. Banks thinks, as the chair was not frequently used, that it was only called into requisition for peculiar cases.

Down to about 1840 a lady named Miss Atherton had a private sedan in Manchester. In addition to the bearers, a footman in livery walked by the side of the chair. This lady was the last person in the place to use a sedan.

The following bye-laws relating to sedans were passed by the Commissioners of Police in Manchester in 1802. " For carrying one person not exceeding 1,000 yards, one shilling; above 1,000 yards and not exceeding one mile, one shilling and sixpence; exceeding a mile and not more than a mile and a half, two shillings;

above a mile and a half and not exceeding two
miles, three shillings.   For short visiting fares
not exceeding 500 yards if brought back, then in
the whole one shilling and sixpence.   Every fare
after   twelve   o'clock   at   night,   except   from
assemblies or balls at the public rooms, to be
doubled ; but from assemblies at the public rooms
after the time last mentioned, only fare and half-
fare to be allowed."

At Blackburn, another Lancashire town, the
sedan was in use down to about 1830.   Very few
persons in the town, says a correspondent of a
local journal, could afford a carriage, so that the
sedan was in request to convey ladies to and from
balls or to the theatre.   " Cabs," it is stated,
" are quite a modern institution in Blackburn, as
many can remember the astonishment which was
created on the introduction of the first cab."

The sedan figures in the amusing pages of
" Pickwick."   It is described as standing in an
old inn-yard, and " having been originally built
for a gouty gentleman with funded property,
would hold Mr. Pickwick and Mr. Tupman at
least as comfortably as a modern post-chaise."
In this chair they were carried in triumph before
the Ipswich magistrates.

Until about 1830, the sedan was popular in Wakefield. John Hewitt, a collector of local history, left on record a note to the effect that "an old sedan, which would hold four persons, was kept in use at the Workhouse down to 1866. It was employed to carry sick persons, and paupers always carried it. Sometimes it was used to carry infirm persons to church."

A Wakefield newspaper for December, 1805, contains an account of an accident occurring to an occupant of a sedan chair. "As a young lady," says the report, "was being carried in a sedan chair from a concert down Westgate at dark, the oil-lamp on the prison wall being out, and the next lamp being nearly 100 yards off, the carriers, being probably rather fresh, missed the Westgate Bridge, and ran the sedan at a trotting pace into the ford. The lady, much alarmed, got on one side of the chair, the two men lost their balance, and the whole were thrown into the water up to their knees. Some help being at hand, the lady was extricated and brought out of the beck, having received no harm except a cold wetting and a little fright."

Another newspaper story which also belongs to the earlier years of the present century, relates how a beauty of the period was on her way in a sedan to a ball in Belgrave Square district, London, when a strange disaster occurred. "It was a wet night," so runs the report, "and the bearers doubled. The chair was frail, its foundations unsound. The extra motion shook it and

THE SEDAN CHAIR.

its substantial contents, who stood up to remonstrate; but suddenly the bottom fell out, and down she came plump, with her feet on the ground. The bearers did not hear her cries of distress, they jog-trotted on, and she with them. Only her silk hosed-legs were seen, even to the garters. In this guise she went down two streets, when the watchman of the district came to her rescue."

It is stated respecting the celebrated Hannah More that in 1784, during the Westminster election, she was carried in a chair from Henrietta Street through Covent Garden, when a great crowd followed her, crying out : " It is Mrs. Fox : none but Mr. Fox's wife would dare to come into Covent Garden in a chair. She is going to canvass in the dark !" " Though not a little frightened," says Hannah, " I laughed heartily at this ; but shall stir out no more in a chair for some time."

A work entitled " The Picture of London for 1802," contains the following " Rates for Chair-men ":-

" For the first hour, if paid by the hour	1s.	6d.
For every hour afterwards …	0	6
For any distance not exceeding one mile …	1	0
For one mile to one mile and a half	1	6
For every half mile afterwards	0	6."

The foregoing are similar to the fares charged by hackney coachmen, and the regulations framed for their guidance were nearly identical. In London, in bygone times, the hackney coachmen and chairmen did not bear high characters. It is

stated in " A view of London ; or, The Strangers
Guide " (1803-4), " the hackney coaches in London
were formerly limited to 1000 ; but by Act of
Parliament, the number is increased. Hackney
coachmen are, in general, depraved characters,
and several of them have been convicted as
receivers of stolen goods." The writer then
suggests that the men should be licensed.
Penalties were inflicted for misconduct, and
attempts were made to protect the public against
these men. Gay had not a high opinion of chairs
and chairmen. He thus warns his reader :—

> " Let not the Chairman with assuming stride,
> Press near the Wall, and rudely thrust thy Side ;
> The Laws have set him Bounds ; his servile Feet
> Should ne'er encroach where Posts defend the Street.
> Yet who the Footman's Arrogance can quell,
> Whose Flambeau gilds the Sashes of Pell Mell ?
> When in long Rank a Train of Torches flame,
> To light the Midnight Visits of the Dame ?
> Others, perhaps, by happier Guidance led,
> May where the Chairman rests, with Safety tread :
> When e'er I pass, then Poles, unseen below,
> Make my Knee tremble with the jarring Blow."

Many of the private chairs were highly
ornamented. Queen Anne presented to the King
of Prussia one valued at £8,000. It was,
perhaps, the finest chair ever made in this country.

Long journeys were sometimes taken in sedans. Princess Amelia, for example, in 1728, was carried by eight chairmen from St. James's to Bath. The time taken was from April 13th to the 19th. The men took turns in carrying, and when not engaged, had a coach drawn by six horses at their disposal.

Mr. Eliezer Edwards, in his volume entitled " Words, Facts, and Phrases " (London, 1882), has two important items on this theme. Mr. Edwards states that the last he remembers to have seen was used by Miss Linwood, celebrated for her magnificent pictures in needlework, one of which she bequeathed to the Queen. She spent her later years at Leicester, and her sedan was frequently seen in the streets of that town about 1840. She died March 2nd, 1845. Mr. Edwards was informed by the Rev. W. K. R. Bedford, of Sutton Coldfield, that at Southwell, Notts., ladies went in sedans to balls in 1849-50.

The chairs at Edinburgh were numerous and in many instances extremely elegant. " Lady Don was about the last person (so far as I recollect)," says Lord Cockburn, in his " Memorials," " in Edinburgh who kept a private chair. Hers stood in the lobby, and was as handsome and comfortable as silk and velvet and gilding could make it. And when she wanted to use it, two well-known respectable chairmen, enveloped in her livery cloaks, were the envy of their brethren. She and Mrs. Rochead both sat in the Tron Church ; and well do I remember how I used to form one of the cluster that always took its station to see these beautiful relics emerge from the coach and chair." Dr. Charles Rogers, in his "Social Life in Scotland," a work issued by the Grampian Club (Edinburgh, 1884), relates that the use of the chairs was confined to Edinburgh. "In Glasgow and other towns," says Rogers, "gentlewomen proceeded to evening parties on foot, muffled in shawls and plaids, and attended by bare-footed hand-maidens. In like fashion they returned home." A letter written in 1787, to Burns by Clarinda, inviting him to tea about eight in the evening, has a reference to the sedan. "I hope," she writes, "you'll come *afoot*, even though you take a chair home. A chair is so uncommon a thing in our neighbourhood it is apt to raise speculation, but they are all asleep by ten." An amusing anecdote about sedans is furnished by Dean Ramsay. He tells how a dowager lady of quality had gone out to dinner in a chair, and while she was being entertained upstairs, her bearers were feasting and drinking downstairs. " When my lady was to return," says the Dean, "and had taken her place in the sedan, her bearers raised the chair ; but she found no progress was made ; she felt herself sway first to one side, and then to the other, and soon came bump to the ground, when Donald behind was heard shouting to Donald before (for the bearers of sedans were always Highlanders), ' Let her down, Donald, man, for she's drunk.' "

For a long period the sedan remained popular among the lovers of refinement. It was brought into the hall, and the lady or gentleman stepped into it, and without the least disarrangement of hair or dress, the occupants were conveyed to places of public entertainment, and on arrival were ready to enter the room without the trouble of consulting a looking-glass.

Running Footmen.

THE running footman survived down to the earlier years of the present century. The Duke of Queensberry, who died in 1810, is said to have been the last of the noblemen of London to keep one of these servants. An amusing anecdote is related by Mr. William J. Thoms, F.S.A., of a man who made application to the duke for a situation. It was the practice, so runs the story, of his Grace to try the paces of the candidates up and down Piccadilly, and from his balcony he watched and timed them. It was customary to dress the applicants in his livery before a trial of their skill was made. On one occasion it is related that a man presented himself, dressed, and ran. At the conclusion of his performance, the duke, addressing him from his balcony, said, "You will do very well for me." The man replied, "And your livery will do very well for me." He then turned his back on the duke, and gave him another proof of his ability as a runner by running away with the livery in which he was attired.

1

Sir Walter Scott saw the stage-coach of John, Earl of Hopetoun, attended by a running footman dressed in white and bearing a long staff.

These men were kept more for show than use. The roads in the olden time were bad, and it usually took an hour for a coach to travel five miles. In some instances the performances were much more rapid. It is recorded that the Duke of Marlborough for a wager drove his carriage and four to Windsor, and just beat one of these men, who died shortly afterwards. " A clever runner," says a writer in Chambers's " Book of Days," " in his best days would undertake to do as much as seven miles an hour, when necessary, and go three-score miles a day ; but, of course, it was not possible for any man to last long who tasked himself in this manner. Mrs. St. George, in her " Journal kept during a visit to Germany, in 1799-1800," has an important note bearing on running footmen. " These unhappy people," she writes, " always precede the carriages of their masters in town, and sometimes even in the suburbs. They seldom live above three or four years, and generally die of consumption. Fatigue and disease are painted in their pallid and drawn features ; but, like victims, they are crowned with

flowers, and adorned with tinsel." It is related in
the " Berkeley Manuscripts" that Langham, an
Irishman who lived in the Berkeley family in the

days of Queen Elizabeth, on one occasion when
Lady Berkeley was sick, "carried a letter from
Callowdon to old Dr. Fryer, a physician dwelling
in Little Britain in London, and returned with a

glass bottle in his hand, compounded by the doctor for the recovery of her health, a journey of 148 miles, performed by him in less than forty-two hours, notwithstanding his stay of one night at the physician's and apothecary's houses, which no one horse could have so well and safely performed; for which the lady shall after give him a new suit of clothes." Many more records similar to the foregoing might be reproduced respecting the feats of these men.

In the familar name of *footman* for a man-servant we keep alive the memory of the ancient office of running-footman. A memorial of this servant is the sign of a public-house, called *The Running-Footman* in Charles Street, Berkeley Square, London. We reproduce a picture of this old-fashioned sign-board. It gives us a good idea of the costume of the fraternity. The outfit varied a little. A contributor to the " Book of Days" describes it as consisting of "a light black cap, a jockey-coat, white linen trousers, or a mere linen shirt coming to the knees, with a pole seven feet long." At the top of the pole was a silver ball, containing, for the use of the man on his journey, white wine and eggs.

Under this heading may be mentioned the

link-boy, who, with his torch of pitch and tow,
preceded the coach or sedan chair at night.

He was in much
request in the West
End of London until
about 1807, when
gas was introduced.
There are many
allusions to the link-
boys in the plays and
the lighter poems of
the last century, and

A LINK-BOY.

often not of a flattering character. They are
described as a disorderly class of men, and many
followed the calling as a cloak for thievery.
Gay, in his "Trivia," says :—

> "Though thou art tempted by the linkman's call,
>   Yet trust him not along the lonely wall :
>   In the midway he'll quench the flaming brand,
>   And share the booty with the pilfering band."

The Early Days of the Umbrella.

THE umbrella is by no means a modern invention. We derive its present name from the Latin *Umbra, a shade*, but long before the Latins had a language or a nation the thing the word represents was a tangible reality. It is shown in ancient Egyptian and Assyrian pictures as a symbol of royalty, being upheld over the heads of kings or rulers of men. But its origin will have been earlier than the existence of a king, will have grown out of the necessity for shade, and its first precursor have been a large leaf upheld by its stalk. The first idea of an umbrella shaped as we know it, must have been suggested by the umbel of a flowering plant.

In the year 1752, Lieutenant-Colonel (afterwards General) Wolfe in a letter from Paris said that "the people here use umbrellas in hot weather to defend them from the sun, and something of the same kind to save them from the snow and rain. I wonder that a practice so useful is not introduced into England." About the time the future conqueror of Quebec wrote his letter, the umbrella had been brought to London.

JONAS HANWAY, THE FIRST ENGLISHMAN WHO EVER CARRIED AN UMBRELLA.

Jonas Hanway, a celebrated traveller and philanthropist, returned to England from Persia in 1750, and in his biography, published in 1787, under the title of " Remarkable Occurrences in the life of Jonas Hanway," by John Pugh, it is stated that Hanway "was the first man who ventured to walk the streets of London with an umbrella over his head. After carrying one nearly thirty years he saw them come into general use."

Long before Hanway's time, ladies had enjoyed the luxury of having an umbrella. In the earlier years of the seventeenth century we find traces of it. Ben Jonson, in his comedy, dated 1616, entitled *The Devil is an Ass*, speaking of an accident which befel a lady at the Spanish Court, says :—

> " And there she lay, flat spread as an umbrella."

Beaumont and Fletcher, in their *Rule a Wife and Have a Wife* (1640), have an allusion to the umbrella as follows :—

> " Are you at ease?   Now is your heart at rest ?
> Now you have got a shadow, an umbrella,
> To keep the scorching world's opinion
> From your fair credit."

Swift, speaking of a city shower, in the *Tatler* in 1710, directs attention to the common use of the umbrella amongst women.   He says :—

> " Now in contiguous drops the flood comes down,
> Threatening with deluge the devoted town ;
> To shops in crowds, the draggled females fly,
> Pretend to cheapen goods, but nothing buy ;

" The Templar spruce, while every spout's abroach,
Stays till 'tis fair, yet seems to call a coach,
The tucked-up sempstress walks with hasty strides,
While streams run down her oiled umbrella's sides."

John Gay, in his " Trivia ; or, The Art of Walking the Streets of London " (1715), says :—

" Underneath th' umbrella's oily shade,"

thus indicating that the umbrellas of that period were made of oiled silk or linen, and that an advance had been made from the flattened form of 1616 to something of the dome-shape in present use. About this period was introduced the custom of keeping an umbrella in the halls of the larger houses, to be used on a wet day when anyone was passing from the door to a carriage. It may be inferred from the following announcement, copied from the *Female Tatler*, of December 12th, 1709, that this useful article was deemed far too effeminate for the use of a man :—" The young gentleman borrowing the umbrella belonging to Wills' Coffee-house, in Cornhill, of the mistress, is hereby advertised, that to be dry from head to foot on the like occasion, he shall be welcome to the maid's pattens."

Horace Walpole, in his account of the punishment of Dr. Shebbeare for libel, December 5th,

1758, records that "the man stood in the pillory, having a footman holding an umbrella to keep off the rain." This has been described as an aristocratic style of bearing punishment. The Under-Sheriff was punished for permitting the indulgence.

A footman named John Macdonald travelled in various parts of the world, and wrote an interesting account of his life and travels. He returned to London in 1778, and brought with him from Spain "a fine silk umbrella." When he used it in the streets he was greeted with derisive shouts of "Frenchman, Frenchman! why don't you call a coach?" The hackney-coachmen and chairmen made the most noise, for they were not slow to recognise that the use of the umbrella would enable people to do without coaches in wet weather, and it was then that their conveyances were in the greatest demand. The coaches were uncomfortable, and when the weather was fine, gentlefolk preferred walking to being jolted in conveyances.

The introduction of the umbrella to many places is recorded in local historical works. Dr. Spens, a popular physician, is said to have been the first man to carry one in Edinburgh, and the year

1779 is set down as the time of its first appearance
in the streets. According to the "Statistical
Account of Glasgow," by Dr. Cleland, "about
the year 1781 or 1782, the late Mr. John Jameson,
surgeon, brought with him an umbrella on his
return from Paris, which was the first seen in the
city, and attracted universal attention. This
umbrella was made of heavy wax-cloth, with cane
ribs, and was a ponderous article." Mr. Jameson
was a man of much humour, and took a delight in
relating stories of the surprise caused by his
umbrella. It was related in a Scotch newspaper
that "when umbrellas were first marched into
Blairgowrie, they were sported only by the
minister and the laird, and were looked upon
by the common class of people as perfect
phenomena. One day Daniel M—— went to
Colonel McPherson, at Blairgowrie House;
when about to return, a shower came on, and the
colonel politely offered him the loan of an
umbrella, which he gladly accepted, and Daniel,
with his head two or three inches higher than
usual, marched off. Not long after he had left,
however, the colonel again saw Daniel posting
towards him with all possible haste, still o'ertopped
by his cotton canopy (silk umbrellas were out of

the question in those days), which he held out,
saluting him with : ' Hae, hae, kornil, this'll never
dae ; there's nae a door in a' ma hoose that'll tak
it in ; ma very barn door winna' tak it in.'"
We glean from a note written for us by Mr.
Andrew James Symington, the well-known author
and antiquary, that his grandfather, William
Symington, towards the close of the last century,
was the first man in Paisley who carried an
umbrella.   It was of large size, and had an extra
handle at the top point by which to hang it up to
dry, so that the water ran down to the points of
the ribs, and off.   This was a sensible practical
arrangement, although it prevented the umbrella
from being used as a staff.   Mr. Symington's
mother told him that in Renfrewshire and
Lanarkshire umbrellas were first used by ladies,
and then men began to use them, but for a
long time as new-fangled oddities and regarded
with curiosity.

The first umbrella ever used in Cartmel, Lancashire, was brought by Mrs. Stockdale in 1776,
from the island of Granada, in the West Indies.
About 1780, a red Leghorn umbrella was introduced into Bristol, and created quite a sensation
among the townsfolk.   It is suggested that it may

have been brought from Leghorn, as ships traded between the two places. It is related that one of the earliest umbrellas seen in Taunton belonged to the clergyman, and when he took it to church he used to hang it in the porch for the edification and delight of his parishioners. The Rev. G. C. Renouard contributed to *Notes and Queries* in 1850 some important information on this theme. He stated as follows :—" In the hall of my father's house at Stamford, Lincolnshire, there was, when I was a child, the wreck of a large green silk umbrella, apparently of Chinese manufacture, brought by my father from Scotland, somewhere between 1770 and 1780, and, I have often heard, it was the first umbrella seen at Stamford. I well remember also an amusing description given by the late Mr. Warry, so many years consul of Smyrna, of the astonishment and envy of his mother's neighbours, at Sawbridgeworth, in Hants, where his father had a country house, when he ran home and came back with an umbrella, which he had just brought from Leghorn, to shelter them from a pelting shower which detained them in the church porch, after the service, on one summer Sunday. From Mr. Warry's age at the time he mentioned this, and

other circumstances in his history, I conjecture
that it occurred not later than 1775 or 1776. As
Sawbridgeworth is so near London, it is
evident that even then umbrellas were almost
unknown."

In the last decade of the last century, and
possibly earlier, Mr. John Daniel, of Manchester,
the maternal grandfather of Mrs. Geo. Linnæus
Banks, the popular novelist, was a manufacturer
of smallwares, umbrellas included. He had a
large trade in them for America. Those shipped
to the United States were mostly of gingham, and
very bright colours, red, green, and blue. They
were made on frames or ribs of stout whalebone,
the stretchers, which served to open and close the
umbrella, were of wrought metal. To prevent the
whalebone splitting, the long-ribs were tipped with
metal (japanned) or ivory, pierced and stitched
through cover and whalebone to secure them.
The ribs were secured to the stick at the top
by wire. It was not until this century that
what is called the "wheel-top" was invented
for the better security of the individual ribs
between the teeth of the wheel. There was
always a long brass ferule at the end of the
stick, having a kind of flange to cover the

junction of the silk or gingham at the top. It was not until the patent tubular metal frames were introduced about 1835-6, that the whalebone ribs, both for umbrellas and parasols, were discarded as heavy and clumsy. They were at all events durable.

Extra large umbrellas with long stout sticks were in use in the early years of this century as gig-umbrellas, the long handle being slipped into a socket in the gig splash-board, thus supplying shelter, yet leaving the driver's hands free.

Umbrellas were provided for clergymen, who, bareheaded, conducted the burial service at the open grave. In old churchwardens' accounts are many items relating to this useful article. The earliest we have noted occurs in the accounts of St. Nicholas' Church, Newcastle-on-Tyne, and are as follow :—

"1717—Paid for an umbrella for the
    churche's use £1 5 0
1717.—Paid Tho. Melburne for charges
    about ye umbrella ...   0 2 0."

In the accounts of Wrexham is an entry :—

"April 2, 1742.—Pd. William Wright, for
    an Umberellow ...   ... £1 1 0."

At Wakefield, Yorkshire, the following items appear in the accounts :—

> "1754, Oct. 19.—Cash paid for one
>   umbrella £2   0   0
>   Box and carriage for umbrella ...   0   4   0."

Writing in 1886, Mr. Geo. Roberts, a painstaking local antiquary, records "that an old lady, still living, was the first to use an umbrella in Wakefield, and that she generally walked along the back streets when carrying the article, to avoid the gaze and the remarks of curious persons, and to avoid the children, who wondered to see such a novelty." At Wakefield a woman was paid for taking charge of the church umbrella. Entries like the following occur in the accounts :—

> "1770, Jan. 2.—Dame Lofthouse, for
>   bringing out the Umbrella ...   £0   5   0
>   „ May 26—Dame Lofthouse, ½ year
>   for Umbrella   0   5   0."

At Leigh, Lancashire, is an entry in the accounts as under :

> "1755—Pd. John Orm's Bill for
>   Umberellow ...   £0   8   6."

From the parish book of Cranbrook, Kent, are the following items : -

> "1783—Pd. for an Umbrella   £0 12   0   .
>   1786—Pd. for an Umbrella   0 15   0."

More entries similar to the foregoing might
be quoted.

In many old books, interesting items respecting
the umbrella occur, and it will, perhaps, not be
without interest to reproduce some of the more
important which have come under our notice.
Florio, in his "Worlde of Wonders," published
in 1598, states:—"Ombrella, a fan, a canopie,
also a testern or cloth of state for a prince, also a
kind of round fan or shadowing that they use to
ride with in summer in Italy, a little shade." A
rare work entitled "Crudities," by Thomas
Coryat, issued in 1611, furnishes a curious
account of the early use of the umbrella in Italy.
The author says:—"Also, many of them" [the
Italians] "do carry other fine things of a far
greater price, that will cost a ducat at least, which
they commonly call in the Italian tongue
umbrellas—that is, things that minister shadow
unto them for shelter against the scorching heat
of the sun. These are made of leather, something answerable to the form of a little canopy,
hooped in the inside, with divers little wooden
hoops, that extend the umbrella in a pretty large
compass. They are used especially by horsemen,
who carry them in their hands when they ride,

K

fastening the end of the handle upon one of the thighs ; and they impart so long a shadow unto them, that it keepeth the heat of the sun from the upper parts of their bodies." Blunt's "Glosso-graphia," published in 1674, states :—"Umbello (Italian), a fashion of round and broad fans, wherewith the Indians (and from them our great ones) preserve themselves from the heat of the sun ; and hence any little shadow, fan, or other thing wherewith the women guard their faces from the sun." Kersey's "Dictionary," issued 1708, describes it thus :—"A broad fan or screen, commonly used by women to shelter them from rain."

Defoe's description of Robinson Crusoe's umbrella is well-known to most readers. It will be remembered that he makes his hero say that he had seen the umbrella in Brazil, where they were used as a protection against the great heats. Crusoe gives an account of the one he made. "I covered it with skins," he says, "the hair out-wards, so that it cast off the rain like a pent-house, and kept off the sun effectually, that I could walk out in the hottest of the weather with greater advantage than I could before in the coolest." From the foregoing description, heavy umbrellas in both England and France were known as Robinsons.

Mr. William Sangster, in compiling his interesting little book entitled " Umbrellas and their History," consulted a large number of works containing matter relating to his subject. The result of his labours is a lasting contribution to historical literature. " Careful research," says Mr. Sangster, "has enabled us to light on a solitary instance of an ancient English umbrella, for Wright, in his ' Domestic Manners of the English,' gives a drawing from the Harleian MSS., No. 603, which represents an Anglo-Saxon gentleman walking out attended by his servant, the servant carrying an umbrella with a handle that slopes backwards, so as to bring the umbrella over the head of the person in front. It probably, therefore, could not be shut up, but otherwise it looks like an ordinary umbrella, and the ribs are represented distinctly."

In the East, the use of umbrellas appears to have been confined to royalty. It was largely carried by the Greeks and Romans, persons of rank.

A Talk about Tea.

THAT genial and gossipy writer, Samuel Pepys, in his Diary, which supplies so much curious and interesting information on bygone days and ways, states that, on September 25, 1660, he sent for his first cup of tea. That was by no means its earliest appearance in London, and it is surprising that Pepys had not previously partaken of it. The year 1660 is, however, memorable in the history of tea, for at this time it became a taxable commodity. A tax of eightpence per gallon was imposed on all tea made for sale ; subsequently the leaf and not the liquid was taxed. The rate of taxation has been changed at various periods ; and the tax has added much to the revenue of the country.

The Dutch brought tea from China to Europe as early as 1610. On its introduction to England the price ranged from £6 to £10 per pound.

In the columns of the *Mercurius Politicus*, under date of September 30, 1658, appeared an advertisement as follows :

" That excellent, and by all Physicians approved, *China* drink called by the Chineans *Tcha*, by other nations *Tay* alias *Tee*, is sold at the Sultaness Head Coffee House, in Sweeting's Rents by the Royal Exchange, London."

About this time, and perhaps prompted by the preceding announcement, Thomas Garway, proprietor of a coffee-house near the Royal Exchange, issued a broadside respecting tea, and a copy is preserved in the Library of the British Museum. We cull as follows from the historically interesting document :—

" The quality is moderately hot, proper for winter or summer. The drink is declared to be most wholesome, preserving in perfect health until extreme old age. The particular virtues are these : It maketh the body active and lusty. It helpeth the headache, giddiness and heaviness thereof. It removeth the obstructions of the spleen. It is very good against the stone and gravel. . . . It taketh away the difficulty of breathing, opening obstructions. It is good against lippitude distillations, and cleareth the sight. It removeth lassitude, and cleanseth and purifieth acrid humours and a hot liver. It is good against crudities, strengthening the weakness of the stomach, causing good appetite and digestion, and particularly for men of corpulent body, and such as are great eaters of flesh. It vanquisheth heavy dreams, easeth the brain, and strengtheneth the memory. It overcometh superfluous sleep, and prevents sleepiness in general, a draught of the infusion being taken ; so that without trouble whole nights may be spent in study without hurt to the body. It prevents and cures agues, surfeits, and fevers by infusing a fit quantity of the leaf, thereby provoking a most gentle vomit and breathing of the pores, and hath been given with wonderful success. It (being prepared and drunk with milk and water) strengtheneth the inward parts and prevents consumptions. . . . It is good for colds, dropsies, and scurvies, and expelleth infection. . . . And that the virtues and excellencies of this leaf and drink are many and great is evident and manifest by the high esteem and use of it (especially of late years) by the physicians and knowing men of France, Italy, Holland, and other parts of Christendom, and in England it hath been sold in the leaf for six pounds, and sometimes for ten pounds, the pound weight ; and in respect of its former scarceness and dearness, it hath been only used as a regalia in high treatments and entertainments, and presents made thereof to princes and grandees till the year 1657. The said Thomas Garway did purchase a quantity thereof, and first publicly sold the said tea in leaf and drink, made according to the directions of the most knowing merchants and travellers in those Eastern countries, and upon knowledge and experience of the said Garway's continued care and industry in obtaining the best tea, and making drink thereof, very many noblemen, physicians, merchants, and gentlemen of quality, have ever since sent to him for the said leaf, and daily resort to his house in Exchange Alley aforesaid, to drink the drink thereof; and to this intent, &c., these are to give notice that the said Thomas hath tea to sell from sixteen to fifty shillings the pound."

Since the days of Garway an almost countless number of tea advertisements have appeared, but we do not think any one surpasses the foregoing in praising the virtues of the "cups that cheer, but not inebriate." It must have greatly impressed the public, and done much to make tea-drinking popular.

Some years passed before tea found its way into the home of Mr. Samuel Pepys. Writing in his "Diary," under date of June 28, 1667, he states :—" Home, and there find my wife making tea, a drink which Mr. Pelling, the potticary, sells her for her cold and defluxions." Charles Knight penned a pleasing paragraph about Mrs. Pepys making her first cup of tea. "How carefully," wrote Knight, "she metes the grains of the precious drug which Mr. Pelling, the potticary, had sold her at an enormous price---a crown an ounce at the very least ; she has boiled the liquor once before, but then there was sugar in the infusion--a beverage only for the highest. If tea should become fashionable, it will cost their housekeeping as much as their claret." She learns with satisfaction that the price of tea is coming down, for he produces Garway's broadside, with its welcome news that Thomas Garway has a large quantity for sale.

Charles II., in 1662, married Princess Catherine of Portugal. She had enjoyed tea in her native land, and on coming to England did much to render it popular here. Edmund Waller, in a Birthday Ode on the Queen, credits her Majesty with the introduction of the herb. His lines are as follow :—

" Venus her myrtle, Phœbe has her bays ;
Tea both excels, which she vouchsafes to praise,
The best of Queens and best of herbes we owe
To that bold nation which the way did show
To the fair region where the sun does rise,
Whose rich productions we so justly prize.
The Muse's friend, tea does our fancy aid,
Repress those vapours which the head invade,
And keep that palace of the soul serene,
Fit on her birthday to salute the Queen."

Waller was a courtly and amatory poet, and is believed to have been the first to write a poem in praise of tea. He is best known as the writer of a song entitled " Go, Lovely Rose," which has gained for him a lasting place in literature.

Dr. Samuel Johnson says that tea was first imported into England from Holland, in the year 1666, by Earls Arlington and Ossory, and that their ladies taught women of quality how to use it. From the preceding facts we see that Johnson's statement is incorrect. We also learn from *Rugge's Diurnal,* that, in 1659, tea was sold in almost every street in London. Two years later the East India Company deemed a couple of pounds of tea a suitable present for the king. A few years later namely, in 1677—the East India Company imported from China 4713 pounds, which glutted the market for several years.

Tea-drinking amongst the rich was fashionable, although with not a few it met with little favour, and in prose and poetry was denounced. We may readily believe, from an entry in the diary of Lord Clarendon, dated 10th February, 1688, that his lordship was not a little proud of his tea. " Le Père Couplet supped with me," says Lord Clarendon. " He is a man of very good conversation. After supper we had tea, which he said was as good as any he had drank in China. The Chinese who came over with him and Mr. Fraser, supped likewise with us." Dean Swift, in the " Journal of a Modern Lady," draws the tea-table as the arena for the ladies to display their capacity for backbiting and scandal. He says :—

> " Let us now survey
> Our madam o'er her evening tea,
> Surrounded with the noisy clans
> Of prudes, coquettes, and harridans.
> Now voices over voices rise,
> While each to be the loudest vies :
> They contradict affirm, dispute,
> No single tongue one moment mute ;
> All mad to speak and none to hearken.
> They set the very lapdog barking ;
> Their chattering makes a louder din
> Than fishwives o'er a cup of gin ;
> Far less the rabble roar and rail
> When drunk on sour election ale."

Young writes in an almost equally unjust strain. He says :—

> "Tea ! how I tremble at thy fatal stream !
> As Lethe dreadful to the love of fame.
> What devastations on thy banks are seen,
> What shades of mighty names that once have been !
> A hecatomb of characters supplies
> Thy painted altars' daily sacrifice."

Another writer, believing in the ways of old, declares :—

> " 'Twas better for each British virgin,
> When on roast beef, strong beer, and sturgeon,
> Joyous to breakfast they sat around,
> Nor were ashamed to eat a pound."

The Earl of Northumberland, in the year 1512, commenced the compilation of a work detailing the every-day life and expenses of Wressel Castle, and his other northern strongholds. From this work we may gather a good idea of the consumption of wine and beer before the advent of tea. The particulars of food in Tudor times are of interest. The number of daily meals was four, consisting of breakfast, taken at seven, dinner at ten, supper at four, and lastly, livery served in the bedroom between eight and nine o'clock, before retiring to rest. On flesh days, the earl and countess had for breakfast a quart of wine, and their two sons one pottle of beer, containing two quarts. On fish days, for breakfast the earl and countess had a quart of beer and a quart of wine. For their liveries they had a gallon of beer and a quart of wine. The wine was warmed and mixed with spices. Particulars are given of quarts of beer being given to children in the nursery, and my lady's gentlewomen had their pottles of beer.

The love of ale even amongst ladies lasted for a long time in England. A good illustration bearing out this matter is mentioned by Dr. Aikin, the historian of Manchester. "About 1720," writes Aikin, "there were not above three or four carriages kept in the town. One of these belonged to Madame ——, in Salford. This respectable old lady was of a social disposition, and could not bring herself to conform to the new-fashioned beverage of tea and coffee ; whenever, therefore, she made her afternoon's visit, her friends presented her with a tankard of ale and a pipe of tobacco. A little before this period, a country gentleman had married the daughter of a citizen of London ; she had been used to tea, and in compliment to her it was introduced by some of her neighbours, but the usual afternoon's entertainment at gentlemen's houses at that time was wet and dry sweetmeats, different sorts of cake and gingerbread, apples, or other fruits in season, and a variety of home made wines." The record regarding the "old lady" of social disposition at Manchester reminds us of an epitaph placed on a grave-stone in Edwalton churchyard, Nottinghamshire, on Mrs. Freland, a lady having considerable property, and who was a rather free liver. She died in 1741, and the couplet is as follows :—

> " She drank good ale, strong punch and wine,
> And lived to the age of ninety-nine."

In the pleasant pages of the "Autobiography" of the Rev. Charles Rogers, LL.D., the eminent Scottish antiquary and author, is an amusing anecdote anent a present of a pound of tea to one of his ancestors at her marriage in 1726. The gift was regarded as a special mark of honour. The bride invited her neighbours to partake of it, "and in preparing the dish," says Dr. Rogers, "boiled the leaves in a saucepan and served them up with butter and condiments. The dish was unpalatable." We have heard of similar mistakes being made in English households in bygone times.

Tea was introduced into Scotland in the year 1682 by the Duke of York. At that time he

was High Commissioner, and held his court at
Holyrood.   It was a long time before tea became
popular in North Britain, and in proof of this
statement it may be observed that Dr. Somerville
carefully inspected the household books of the
Duke of Queensberry from 1697 to 1708 without
finding any mention of tea.   For some time it
was mainly used as a medicine.   Towards the
close of the sixteenth century an Edinburgh
merchant received a chest of Bohea, costing him
£225 15s., being 15s. per pound.   The price
advanced in 1705.   Bohea was sold at 30s. a
pound, and green tea at 16s.   Ten years later the
price of a pound was 25s.

   When the consumption of tea was increasing in
Scotland, it was feared by some of the leading
men of the country that its use might cause
national effeminacy.   Lord President Forbes
attempted to suppress the tea trade.   He directed
the county magistrates and civic corporations to
denounce the traffic.   It is recorded that in 1743,
"by the Convention of Burghs, the consumption
of tea was associated with the use of foreign
spirits, and classed with it as a national evil.
They passed a resolution complaining 'of the
unhappy circumstances to which this part of the

United Kingdom is reduced by the universal and excessive use of tea and foreign spirits to which all ranks, even the very meanest of the people, are tempted by the low prices at which such commodities are afforded by the smuggler.'" This was followed up by a petition to Parliament praying that "the universal and excessive use of tea and foreign spirits" might be prevented.

Here is a copy of a ludicrous resolution respecting the use of tea, passed in 1744, by the tenants of William Fullarton, of Fullarton :—

" We, being all farmers by profession, think it needless to restrain ourselves formally from indulging in that foreign and consumptive luxury called tea; for when we consider the slender constitutions of many of the higher rank, amongst whom it is used, we conclude that it be but an improper diet to qualify us for the more robust manly parts of our business ; and therefore we shall only give our testimony against it, and leave the enjoyment of it altogether to those who can afford to be weak, indolent, and useless."

Several well-meaning people opposed the use of tea on economical grounds.   A contributor to the *Female Spectator*, for 1745, who regarded the snuff-box as a pretty trinket for the lady's pocket,

says that the tea-table "costs more to support than
would maintain two children at nurse; it is the
utter destruction of all economy, the bane of good
housewifery, and the source of idleness." A year
later—namely, on July 6, 1746—John Wesley
gave up the use of tea, and persuaded his followers
to imitate his conduct. Two years later he
published a booklet, bearing the title of " A Letter
to a Friend concerning Tea."

He speaks of tea in the work as "impairing
digestion, unstringing the nerves, involving great
and useless expense." Mr. Wesley also thought
that in his case and in that of others it induced
symptoms of paralysis. It was not because Mr.
Wesley believed that tea-drinking was injurious
that he gave it up in the first instance, but on
account of its cost, and at a time when he wished
to practise rigid economy.

A paper in *The World*, for 1753, describes a
model country rector, and in it is an allusion to
this subject. "His only article of luxury," says
the writer, "is tea, but the doctor says he would
forbid that, if his wife could forget her London
education. However, they seldom offer it but to
the best company, and less than a pound will last
a twelvemonth."

The marked frugality of the worthy rector is a strange contrast to the mistaken extravagance shown when the first pound of tea reached Penrith. It was sent as a present, and without any directions for preparing it. Southey records how some lady friends were invited to enjoy the novelty, and that "they boiled the whole at once in a kettle, and sat down to eat the leaves with butter and salt; and they wondered how any person could like such a dish."

Jonas Hanway, so well remembered as being the first person to carry an umbrella in London, was a persistent opponent of the use of tea. In a large volume, published in 1756, called "A Journal of Eight Days' Journey from Portsmouth to Kingston-upon-Thames, to which is added an Essay on Tea, considered as pernicious to Health, obstructing industry and impoverishing the Nation," he stated his belief that the greater number of feminine disorders resulted from the use of tea, and that it deprived women of their beauty and men of vigour.

It is perhaps the most intemperate essay ever written on the subject. Dr. Johnson, one of the most celebrated devotees of the cup, reviewed the work in the *Literary Magazine*, and a powerful defence of the use of tea might have been expected; but he produced an unsatisfactory criticism, and it has been truthfully described as "weak and lukewarm." Johnson commenced by observing that Hanway "is to expect little justice from a hardened and shameless tea-drinker, who has for twenty years diluted his meals with only the infusion of this fascinating plant; whose kettle has scarcely time to cool; who with tea amuses the evening, with tea solaces the midnight, and with tea welcomes the morning." It is not a little surprising that Johnson did not write with greater force on the beverage he so dearly loved. He has been called "the king of tea-drinkers." "I suppose," said Boswell, "that no person ever enjoyed with more relish the infusion of that fragrant leaf than Johnson. The quantities which he drank, at all hours, were so great, that his nerves must have been uncommonly strong not to have been extremely relaxed by such an intemperate use of it, but he assured me he never felt the least inconvenienced from it."

De Quincey dearly loved his tea. "From the latter weeks of October to Christmas Eve," he writes in his *Confessions*, "is the period during which happiness is in season—in my judgment, enters the room with the tea-tray; for tea, though ridiculed by those who are, of course, nervous, or are become so from wine-drinking, and are not susceptible of influence from so refined a stimulant, will always be the favourite beverage of the intellectual; and for my part, I would have joined Dr. Johnson in a *bellum internecinum* against Jonas Hanway, or any other impious person who should presume to disparage it."

William Howitt, another celebrated man of letters, and pedestrian, wrote warmly in favour of tea. "After long continued exertion, as in the great pedestrian journeys that I formerly made, tea would always, in a manner almost miraculous, banish all my fatigue, and diffuse through my whole frame comfort and exhilaration without any subsequent ill-effect." Mr. George R. Sims, poet and dramatist, finds tea equally refreshing. "Tea," says Mr. Sims, "is my favourite tonic when I am tired or languid, and always has a stimulating effect." He writes :—

"In trying from all things our lips to debar,
Hasn't Science just gallop'd his hobby too far?
Let the nervous go thirsting, they shan't frighten me
With this nonsense concerning milk, water, and tea."

Lord Palmerston refreshed himself at the night

sittings of Parliament with the cheering cup of tea. "Mr. Gladstone," says Mr. Arthur Reade, in his pleasantly compiled work on "Tea and Tea-Drinking," "confessed a short time ago, at Cannes, that he drank more tea between midnight and four in the morning than any other member of the House of Commons; and, strange to say, the strongest tea, although taken immediately before going to bed, never interferes with his sleep." Mr. Justin McCarthy believes that tea-drinking is beneficial, and practises what he preaches by taking a liberal supply of it. He declares it keeps off his only malady—headache.

Around the tea-table gather the happiest memories of our lives. The celebrated Sydney Smith exclaimed :—" Thank God for tea! What would the world do without tea? I am glad I was not born before tea." Our readers will, we feel sure, echo the sentiments of Sydney Smith.

Concerning Coffee.

WE are told that in the year 1641, coffee was introduced into this country by Nathaniel Canopus, a Cretan. He is recorded to have made it a common beverage at Balliol College, Oxford. Prior to the year 1641, mention of it was made in the works of English authors. Lord Bacon, in his *Sylva Sylvarum; or, a Naturall Historie in ten Centuries*, published by W. Rawley, D.D., in 1627, has an interesting note respecting this subject. "They have in Turkey," writes Bacon, "a drink called coffee, made of a berry of the same name, as black as soot, and of a strong scent, but not aromatical, which they take beaten into powder, in water, as hot as they can drink it; and they take it, and sit at it in their coffee-houses, which are like our taverns. The drink comforteth the brain and heart, and helpeth digestion." Burton, in his "Anatomy of Melancholy," published in 1621, speaks of the Turks in their coffee-houses, and observes that these places much resemble our taverns. The antiquity of coffee as a beverage is by no means remote. If there is not age, there is certainly dignity in the origin of the pleasant cup. According to the Mahomedans, coffee was a special revelation of the angel Gabriel to Mahomet, and provides the faithful followers of the prophet with a drink in place of wine, which is condemned by their religion. Such is one of several traditions respecting coffee as a drink.

Its early use as a beverage is obscure, but has been traced to the Persians. About the middle of the fifteenth century it was largely drunk in Arabia Felix ; from thence it passed into Egypt, Syria, and Turkey. At Constantinople, in 1551, a coffee-house was opened. In 1662 it was introduced into France, by a traveller named Thevenot. This was twenty-one years later than the time it was first consumed at Oxford. In 1650 was set up by a Jew, named Jacobs, the first coffee-house in England. Wood speaks of some who " delighted in the noveltie."

Mr. Daniel Edwards, a merchant who had dealings with Turkey, brought to London, in 1652, a bag of coffee and a Greek servant named Pasqua Rosee. Two years later, in St. Michael's Alley, Cornhill, the Greek opened the first coffee-

house established in London   Oldys left a MS.
giving particulars of the origin of the coffee-
house.   He relates how the Ragusan youth used
to prepare coffee for Edwards every morning,
which was deemed a great novelty. " But the
novelty thereof," says Oldys, "drawing too much
company to him, he allowed his said servant, with
another of his son-in-laws, to sell it publicly ;
and they set up the first coffee-house in
London."

This movement commenced in the days of the
Commonwealth ; but we are assured by one who
has carefully studied the history of this eventful
period, that "the Puritans did not abandon their
black-jacks and flasks of strong waters for coffee."
Handbills were the usual mode of advertising at
this time, and one was issued by Rosee.

In the British Museum is still preserved one of
his original broadsides, and it will not be without
interest to give a copy of it :—

"THE VERTUE OF THE COFFEE DRINK,
First made and publickly sold in England by
PASQUA ROSEE.

The grain or berry called coffee, groweth upon little trees
only in the deserts of Arabia. It is brought from thence and
drunk generally throughout all the Grand Seignour's
dominions. It is a simple innocent thing, composed into a

drink by being dried in an oven, and ground to powder, and boiled up with spring water, and about half a pint of it to be drunk fasting an hour before, and not eating an hour after, and to be taken as hot as can possibly be endured ; the which will never fetch the skin of the mouth, or raise any blisters by reason of that heat.

The Turk's drink at meals and other times is usually water, and their diet consists much of fruit ; the crudities whereof are very much corrected by this drink.

The quality of this drink is cold and dry ; and though it be a drier, yet it neither heats nor inflames more than hot posset. It so encloseth the orifice of the stomach, and fortifies the heat within, that it is very good to help digestion, and therefore of great use to be taken about three or four o'clock afternoon, as well as in the morning. It much quickens the spirits, and makes the heart lightsome ; it is good against sore eyes, and the better if you hold your head over it and take in the steam that way. It suppresseth fumes exceedingly, and therefore is good against the head-ache, and will very much stop any defluxion of rheums that distil from the head upon the stomach, and so prevent and help consumptions and the cough of the lungs.

It is excellent to prevent and cure the dropsy, gout, and scurvy. It is known by experience to be better than other drying drink for people of years, or children that have any running humours upon them, as the king's evil, &c. It is a most excellent remedy against the spleen, hypochondriac winds, and the like. It will prevent drowsiness, and make one fit for business, if one have occasion to watch, and therefore you are not to drink of it after supper, unless you intend to be watchful, for it will hinder sleep for three or four hours.

It is observed that in Turkey, where this is generally drunk, that they are not troubled with stone, gout, dropsy, or

scurvy, and that their skins are exceeding clear and white. It
is neither laxative nor restringent.

*Made and Sold in St. Michael's-alley, in Cornhill, by
Pasqua Rosee, at the sign of his own head."*

Notwithstanding much opposition, coffee soon
became a popular drink in England, and had a
marked influence on the progress of civilisation.
Its introduction may be regarded as a step
towards refinement and temperance. The coffee-
houses provided places for the public to meet
away from the taverns with their company excited
by the consumption of beer and spirits.

Shortly after Pasqua Rosee issued his famous
handbill anent "The Vertue of the Coffee
Drink," there was published "A Broadside
against Coffee." It states that Rosee's partner,
the servant of Mr. Edward's son-in-law, was a
coachman. It contradicts the statement that hot
coffee will not burn the mouth, and in an amusing
manner ridicules the broken English of the
Ragusan. We cull from the publication as
follows :—

> " A coachman was the first (here) coffee made,
> And ever since the rest drive on the trade :
> ' *Me no good Engalash !* ' and sure enough,
> He played the quack to salve his Stygian stuff :
> ' *Ver boon for ae stomach, de cough, de phthisick,*'
> And I believe him, for it looks like physic.

" Coffee a crust is charred into a coal,
   The smell and taste of the mock china bowl ;
   Where huff and puff, they labour out their lungs,
   Lest, Dives-like, they should bewail their tongues.
   And yet they tell ye that it will not burn,
   Though on the jury blisters you return ;
   Whose furious heat does make the waters rise,
   And still through the alembics of your eyes,
   Dread and desire, you fall to't snap by snap,
   As hungry dogs do scalding porridge lap.
   But to cure drunkards it has got great fame ;
   Posset or porridge, will't not do the same ?
   Confusion hurries all into one scene,
   Like Noah's ark, the clean and the unclean.
   And now, alas ! the drench has credit got,
   And he's no gentleman that drinks it not ;
   That such a dwarf should rise to such a stature !
   But custom is but a remove from nature.
   A little dish and a large coffee-house,
   What is it but a mountain and a mouse ? "

In spite of poetry and prose being levelled
against coffee-houses, they rapidly increased.
Here people were able to spend a pleasant evening
at a small cost. All sorts and conditions of men
visited the place daily to learn the news and
discuss it. The Stuarts were never in favour of
free speech, and the discussions here were
regarded with unfriendly feeling. A proclamation
"for the suppression of coffee-houses," bearing
date of December 20, 1675. was issued. The

plea for issuing it was because "the multitude of coffee-houses, lately set up and kept within this kingdom, and the great resort of idle and dissipated persons to them, have produced very evil and dangerous effects, particularly in spreading rumours and inducing tradesmen to neglect their calling, tending to the danger of the commonweal, by the idle waste of time and money." It therefore orders all coffee-house keepers, "that they, or any of them, do not presume from and after the tenth day of January next ensuing, to keep any publick coffee-house, or utter, or sell by retail, in his or her house, or houses (to be spent and consumed within the same) any coffee, chocolate, sherbett, or tea; as they will answer it at their utmost peril." A petition was prepared by merchants and retailers of coffee, and presented to Parliament, and resulted in allowing the houses to be kept open six more months. The keepers of the houses were directed to prevent "all scandalous papers, books, and libels from being read in them; and hinder every person from declaring, uttering, or divulging all manner of false and scandalous reports against government or ministers thereof." The proposal was too absurd to receive serious consideration, and those who proposed the proclamation were laughed to scorn. The Government very wisely let it drop.

Here the real history of coffee ends. It is a beverage which retains a lasting hold on the people of England.

The Horn-Book.

"When little children first are brought to schoole,
A horne-booke is a necessary toole."---

Pasquil's Night Cap, 1612.

THE Horn-Book, that ancient medium of scholastic instruction through which our forefathers obtained their rudimentary knowledge of the ABC, was in use before the introduction of printing, and came down to the early years of the present century. At one time it was to be found in every school in the land : it is now a rarity so great as never to be seen save in the interior of a museum, or in the hands of a few collectors of curiosities. To show the extreme scarcity of this old educational primer, we may mention that some time ago an advertisement for one was inserted several times in a leading newspaper without eliciting a response. About thirty years since a Horn-Book was put up at Southgate's Auction-Rooms, London, and actually realised nearly twenty pounds.

So little is known of the use and the history of this relic of the days of yore, that a few notes

on the subject can hardly fail to entertain our
readers. The oldest examples consisted of a
sheet of vellum, with the characters in writing ;
but this primitive form was, on the introduction
of the printing press, changed to a printed
sheet of paper. This was placed on a thin piece
of oak, and over it was laid a sheet of transparent
horn, secured in its position by tacks driven
through a border or mounting of brass. It
usually contained the alphabet in large and small
letters, the Lord's Prayer, and the Roman
numerals. A few monosyllables were occasionally included. The letters in the earlier horn-
books were placed in the form of a Latin cross, A
being at the top, and Z at the bottom ; but
subsequently this was succeeded by the line form,
crosses being figured at the commencement to
remind the young pupil that "The fear of the
Lord is the beginning of wisdom." It was from
the cross ornamentation that it not infrequently
derived the designation of " Christ-cross-row," or
" Chriss-cross-row." Students of Shakespeare
will remember that in *Richard III.* occurs the
following passage :—

> " He hearkens after prophecies and dreams,
> And from the cross-row plucks the letter G."

In *Love's Labour's Lost* allusions to the horn-book likewise appear, and among the old dramatists and poets who refer to it was Ben Jonson, who says :—

> "The letters may be read through the horn,
>   That makes the story perfect."

William Shenstone, the poet, who was placed in his childhood at a dame-school at Halesowen, in Shropshire, was taught his letters from the horn-book. Adverting to the circumstance, in the poem entitled "The School-mistress," included in his volume published in 1737, he thus writes :—

> "Lo! now with state she utters her command;
>   Eftsoons the urchins to their tasks repair;
>   Their books of stature small they take in hand,
>   Which with pellucid horn secured are
>   To save from fingers wet the letters fair."

Thomas Tickell wrote "A Poem in Praise of the Horn-Book," published in 1749, and from this effusion the following lines are culled :—

> "Thee will I sing, in comely wainscot bound,
>   And golden verge inclosing thee around;
>   The faithful horn before, from age to age,
>   Preserving thy invulnerable page;
>   Behind, thy patron saint in armour shines,
>   With sword and lance to guard the sacred lines.
>   Th' instructive handles at the bottom fixed,
>   Lest wrangling critics should pervert the text."

In a poetic composition by William Cowper, there is a description of the horn-book used in his day. His lines are as follow :—

> " Neatly secured from being soil'd or torn,
>   Beneath a pane of thin translucent horn,
>   A book (to please us at a tender age
>   'Tis call'd a book, though but a single page)
>   Presents the prayer the Saviour deign'd to teach,
>   Which children use, and parsons—when they preach."

Prior's lines, which follow, are perhaps more familiar to the general reader than the foregoing quotations :—

> "To Master John the English maid
> A horn-book gives of gingerbread ;
> And, that the child may learn the better,
> As he can name, he eats the letter."

The juveniles, it appears, had their horn-books suspended from the girdle, often learning their lessons without untying the alphabetic charms. That this was the mode of attachment adopted is testified by several old plays which contain allusions to the practice. In a "View of the Beau Monde," printed in 1731, a description of a lady is given as "dressed like a child, in a bodice coat and leading strings, with a horn-book tied to her side."

Black-letter horn-books are extremely rare.

We give a carefully-executed illustration of a fine example found in pulling down an old farm-house at Middleton, Derbyshire. On the back of this

HORN-BOOK—SEVENTEENTH CENTURY.

specimen was a picture of Charles I. in armour, mounted on a horse, thus affording a proof of the period to which it belonged. Generally the

M

patron saint was figured on the reverse of the horn-book, and he is referred to by Tickell in his verses.

Horn-books do not appear to have been very costly, for in the early part of the last century they were sold at the low rate of twopence each. Mr. Halliwell, in his edition of Shakespeare, quotes the following item from the accounts of the Archer family :—" Jan. 8, 1735 : one Horn-book for Mr. Eyres, 00 : 00 : 02." In a bill, dated 1734, a horn-book gilt is put down at the same price. In a quaint old publication by Peacham, entitled " The worth of a Penny," it is recorded :— " For a penny you may buy the hardest book in the world, at which at some time or other hath posed the greatest clerks in the land, viz., an horn-book, the making up of which employs above thirty trades."

We cannot close this brief paper without re-chronicling an instance of ready wit credited to one of our highest legal luminaries. Thus runs the anecdote :—A learned judge, enquiring of Lord Erskine if a single sheet could be called a book, that ready-witted and able representative of the law promptly replied, " The common horn-book, my lord."

Fighting=Cocks in Schools.

IT is highly probable that the Romans introduced cock-fighting into England. This
cruel sport was for a long period extremely
popular amongst men and boys. One of the
earliest, if not the first, account of the pastime
being practised by school-boys occurs in a
" Description of the City of London," by William
Fitzstephen, who wrote in the reign of Henry
II., and died in the year 1191. He records that
it was the annual custom on Shrove Tuesday for
the boys to bring to the schools their gamecocks,
to turn the schoolrooms into cockpits, the masters
and pupils spending the morning in witnessing
the birds fight.

In many instances teachers derived much of
their income from payments made by their boys
for providing fighting-cocks for this cruel and
barbarous amusement. The masters generally
claimed as their perquisites the runaway birds and
those killed in battle. Our old school regulations
and accounts contain many allusions to this

subject. In the town accounts of Congleton is a payment: " 1601. Payd John Wagge for dressynge the schoolhouse at the great [Congleton] cock-fyghte, o. o. 4." Wreay School, on the banks of Windermere Lake, was famous for this pastime. Mr. Graham, a Westmoreland squire, bequeathed to the school a silver bell, to be fought for every year. "About three weeks previous to Shrove Tuesday," says a well-informed writer, "the boys fixed upon two of their schoolfellows for captains, whose parents were able and willing to bear the expense of the approaching contest; and the master, on entering school, was saluted by the boys throwing up their caps and the exclamation of 'Dux! Dux!' After an early dinner on Shrove Tuesday, the two captains, attended by their friends and schoolfellows, who were distin-guished by blue and red ribbons, marched in procession from their respective homes to the village green, where each produced three cocks; and the bell was appended to the hat of the victor, in which manner it was handed down from one successful captain to another." This custom lingered until 1836.

A clergyman informed Mr. William Henderson, for publication in his " Folklore of the Northern

Counties of England," issued in 1879, that when he was a scholar at Sedbergh Grammar School, Yorkshire, the master used to be entitled to four-pence-halfpenny yearly from every boy on Shrove Tuesday for purchasing a fighting-cock. "At Heversham, near Milnthorpe," says Mr. Henderson, "the cockpit was in existence close to the school a few years ago." The regulations of the Kendal Grammar School provided that it "be free to all the boys resident in the parish of Kendal, for classics alone, excepting a voluntary payment of a cock-penny, as aforetime, at Shrove-tide, etc." At the grammar school of Grange-over-Sand, it appears from a local historian that gratuitous payment was expected from the parents of each pupil. It varied in amount according to the social standing of the parents, and at the commencement of the present century ranged from two shillings and sixpence to five pounds. The money was known as cockpence, and doubt-less originated with the old practice of providing gamecocks.

Debits of fighting-cocks often formed important items in old school accounts. Here is an example drawn from Sir James Mackintosh's bill, from the master of Fortrose School: "1776-7.

To cocks'-fight dues for 2 years 2s. 6d. each,
5s. od."

The Duke of York, in the year 1681, introduced
the sport into Scotland. Two years later, a cock-
pit was set up at Leith, and it attracted so much
attention that, in 1704, the town-council of
Edinburgh prohibited it as "an impediment to
business." After much debate, it was finally
agreed to confine the sport at Leith to one day
yearly. The barbarous pastime soon became
popular in schools, and masters managed to profit
by it. In Sir John Sinclair's "Statistical Account
of Scotland," published in 1792, in an article by the
minister of Applecross, county of Ross, it is stated
the schoolmaster's income is "composed of two
hundred merks, with 1s. 6d. and 2s. 6d. per quarter
from each scholar; and the cock-fight dues, which
are equal to one quarter's payment from each
scholar." The Rev. Dr. Edgar, in his "Old Church
Life in Scotland," referring to the school at
Mauchline, states that "the owners of these cocks
paid to the schoolmaster a small sum in name of
entry money; and those who did not provide a com-
batant had to pay an extra sum for admission to
the spectacle. It was a gala day in the schoolmaster's calendar, for not only had he the benefit

of pocketing the entry and admission money, but had the privilege of picking up the carcases of the slain and seizing the persons of the fugitives." "Daddy Auld" stopped the sport at Mauchline in the year 1782. It was continued in other schools to a much later time.

Hugh Miller, the famous geologist, who was born in the year 1802, in his popular volume "My Schools and Schoolmasters," gives a graphic account of the amusement in the Cromarty grammar school where he received his education. "The school," says Miller, "like almost all other grammar schools of the period in Scotland, had its yearly cock-fight, preceded by two holidays and a half, during which the boys occupied themselves in collecting and bringing up the cocks. And such always was the array of fighting birds mustered on the occasion, that the day of the festival from morning till night used to be spent in fighting out the battle. For weeks after it had passed the school floor continued to retain its deeply stained blotches of blood, and the boys would be full of exciting narratives regarding the glories of gallant birds who had continued to fight until their eyes had been pecked out ; or who, in the moment of victory, had dropped dead in the middle of the cock-pit." Miller at some length denounces the cruel sport.

Church bells were often rung in England in honour of winning cocks. Kings frequently attended the battles. Henry VIII. encouraged the sport, and James I. greatly enjoyed it. Cromwell prohibited it in the year 1658; but no sooner had the Second Charles ascended the throne than it was revived, and under royal favour was a popular diversion, and battles were fought in most unlikely places. It is stated in the parish register of Hemingborough, Yorkshire, as follows:—" Feb. 2, 1661. Upon fastene day last they came with their cocks to the church, and faught them in the church—namely Thos. Middleton, of Cliff, John Coats, Ed. Widhouse, and John Batley."

Several attempts were made to check this cruel pastime, and it was finally prohibited in the year 1849.

In the days of old, throwing at cocks was a popular sport. Its origin is almost lost in the dim historic past. Some writers trace it back to the time when the Danes ruled England. The foreign masters were hard on the Saxons, and held them in a subjection as bad as

slavery. The inhabitants of an English city
determined to make a bold attempt for freedom,
and formed a conspiracy against the Danes who
were placed over them. It was resolved that
on a certain dark winter's night a dozen brave
men should secretly repair to the town-house,

COCK-THROWING.

overpower the guard, and seize the arms which
were kept there. When that had been effected,
a signal was to be made, and the English were
to leave their houses and slay the invaders. The
operations had no sooner been commenced, than
the noise made disturbed the cocks roosting in the
building, and a loud crowing was the result. The

unusual circumstance put the guard on the alert, who speedily ended the well-planned scheme of liberty. The Danes, it is said, doubled their cruelty to the conspirators.

After the English were freed from the Danish yoke, they are said to have instituted in the city the sport of throwing at cocks, in revenge for the misery their crowing had occasioned. The pastime became popular, and soon spread throughout the land. Shrove Tuesday was set apart for the sport, being the day the effort was made to murder the Danes. In course of time, cock-throwing became an amusement recognised by parish officials, and it frequently figures in old accounts. The profits from the sport were frequently given to the churchwardens for the relief of the poor. The parish accounts of Pinner, near Harrow-on-the-Hill, may be quoted as an example : " 1622. Received from the cocks at Shrovetide, 12s. 0d.   1628. Received for cocks in Toune, 19s. 0d.   Out of Toune, 0s. 6d."

The cock was tied with a piece of string to a stake driven into the ground, and a small sum was charged for throwing at it with short clubs.   In later times, three throws for threepence was the ordinary price.   If the marksman killed the bird, or knocked it down and ran and caught it before it regained its feet, it became his property. The cocks were trained to evade the blows of the throwers. It was a common practice for school-masters to provide cocks for the diversion of their pupils. Kings even engaged in the sport. In a copy of some household accounts we read : "March 2, 7 Hen. VII. Item to Master Bray for rewards to them that brought cokhes at Shrove-tide to Westminster, xxs."

Many attempts were made to stop this sport. There is a charge of 2s. 6d. in the corporation accounts of Worcester in 1745, for crying down cock-throwing. A paragraph in the *Northampton Mercury*, of February, 1788, states : "We can-not but express our wishes that persons in power, as well as parents and masters of families, would exert their authority in suppressing a practice too common at this season of the year—throwing at cocks, a custom which, to the credit of civilised people, is annually declining." It lingered until a late period in many parts of the country, and was finally prohibited. At Wakefield, the magistrates stopped it about the year 1865.

Bull=baiting.

THE baiting of animals may be traced back to an early period in our history. It was a favourite amusement of the Egyptians, the Greeks, the Romans, and other ancient nations.

In England during the Middle Ages the sport was extremely popular, and was patronised from the highest to the lowest in the land. Almost every town and village in the country had its bull-ring. Fitzstephen, a monk of Canterbury, in his description of London in the twelfth century, relates that the city youths on holidays were entertained by the baiting of bulls with dogs.

Baiting animals was a pastime by no means confined to the youth of the country. There are many records of kings, queens, and the most learned men of bygone times enjoying the sport. Queen Elizabeth took a keen delight in the diversion. Soon after her accession to the throne, on May 25th, 1559, she entertained the French ambassadors to dinner, and subsequently the queen and her guests witnessed the baiting of a number of bulls and bears. The next day the ambassadors went by water to the famous Paris Gardens, and were entertained with "another baiting of bulls and bears." In 1586, her majesty received at Greenwich the Danish ambassador, and bull and bear-baiting were provided for his amusement. Towards the close of her reign, the queen entertained another set of ambassadors at the cock-pit near St. James's with the baiting of animals. The queen's life includes many other allusions to her love of this sport. It has been said of Elizabeth that "she loved bear and bull-baiting in public, and amused herself with performing apes in private."

During the Commonwealth the brutal pastime was prohibited, not, if we are to believe Macaulay, on account of the pain inflicted on the animals, but because it gave pleasure to the spectators.

On the re-establishment of the Stuarts on the throne, bull-baiting and other kindred sports once more became popular with the people. We may infer from the writings of Pepys and Evelyn that the more thoughtful of our countrymen did not fail to condemn the amusement. Samuel Pepys, writing in his diary, under date of August 14th, 1666, says, "After dinner, with my wife and Mercer to the Beare-garden, where I had not been, I think, for many years, and saw some good sport of the bulls tossing of the dogs—one into the very boxes. But it is a very rude and nasty pleasure." John Evelyn, F.R.S., the writer of a diary of lasting interest, and a man of most exemplary character and attainments of a high order, refers to this subject. On June 16th, 1670, he states, " I went with some friends to the Bear Gardens, where was cock-fighting, dog-fighting, bear and bull-baiting, it being a famous day for all these butcherly sports, or rather barbarous cruelties. The bulls did exceedingly well, but the Irish wolf-dog exceeded, which was a tall greyhound—a stately creature indeed, who beat the cruel mastiff. One of the bulls tossed a dog full into a lady's lap as she sat in one of the boxes at a considerable height from the arena. Two poor dogs were killed, and so all ended with the ape on horseback, and I was most heartily weary of the rude and dirty pastime, which I had not seen, I think, in twenty years before."

In the days of William III., Misson, a French advocate, visited England, and wrote a graphic account of bull-baiting. "They tie a rope," says Misson, "to the root of the horns of the bull, and fasten the other end of the cord to an iron ring fixed to a stake driven into the ground, so that, the cord being about fifteen feet long, the bull is confined to a space of about thirty feet diameter. Several butchers or other gentlemen, that are desirous to exercise their dogs, stand round about, each holding his own by the ears, and when the sport begins they let loose one of their dogs." He goes on to describe how frequently the dogs are tossed high into the air by the bull and killed, or how the bull is severely bitten by the dogs.

Coming down to the reign of Queen Anne, we find the pastime still retains a hold of the people. Here are copies of two advertisements belonging to this period. The first states that :—

"At the bear-garden in Hockley-in-the-Hole, near Clerkenwell Green, this present Monday, there is a great Match to be fought by two dogs of Smithfield Bars against two dogs of Hampstead, at the 'Reading Bulls,' for one guinea to be spent; five let-goes out of hand, which goes fairest and furthest in wins all; there are two bear-dogs, to jump three jumps apiece at the bear, which jumps highest for ten shillings to be spent. Also variety of bull-baiting and bear-baiting; it being a day of general sport by all the old gamesters, and a bull-dog to be drawn up with fireworks. Beginning at three o'clock."

The second advertisement is to the following effect :—

"At William Wells' bear-garden, in Tuttle fields, Westminster, this present Monday, there will be a green bull baited, and twenty dogs to fight for a collar, and the dog that runs furthest and fairest wins the collar ; with other diversions of bull and bear-baiting. Beginning at two of the clock."

Municipal authorities sanctioned bull-baiting, or to speak more correctly enforced it. It was the duty of mayors to see that there were plenty of animals provided for the purpose of being baited. The town books of Leicester contain numerous references to this subject. It is stated in the records that at a meeting held at the Common Hall, on the Thursday before the feast of Saints Simon and Jude, the following order was made, that "no butcher kill a bull to sell within the town before it is baited." If the regulation was disregarded, the offender was liable to the forfeiture of the dead animal. At Chesterfield,

Derbyshire, any butcher killing a bull in the shambles was compelled to have it baited in the market place, or pay a fine of 3s. 4d.

This recreation was popular at Preston, Lancashire, according to Anthony Hewitson, the local historian, even in Puritanic times. He says : " In 1656, the Corporation bought a bull, primarily for freemen's cattle, and afterwards for baiting purposes, according to custom, in the Market-place."

It was a part of the mayor's duty at Southampton in past times to provide plenty of bulls and bears for baiting. At Winchester, in the records of the city, are several important notes bearing on this topic. We find it stated that certain butchers were ordered to find bulls to be baited, and the other butchers were directed to pay sixpence each yearly towards maintaining the custom. The mayors appear to have transferred the site of baiting from the bull-ring of the city to the vicinity of their own houses. The citizens felt that this was an infringement on their rights, and finally, on the 19th November, 30th Henry VIII., the corporation made an order " That from henceforthe ther shal be no bulstake set before any Mayor's doore to bayte any bull, but onlie at the bull-ringe within the said cytie."

Old municipal and constables' accounts contain numerous items relating to bull-baiting. In the corporation accounts of Exeter is a payment :—

> "1697. Paid John Huntback for a large
>   bull-ring and staple at the Cross,
>   at 4d. per lb.   -   -   -   - 4s. 6d."

Mr. W. H. Dawson, the historian of Skipton, Yorkshire, tells us that the clerk of the market was paid a shilling per annum for taking charge of the bull rope. The following are items reproduced from the old constables' accounts of Skipton :—

> "1734. Oct. 2. Paid for keeping ye bull
>   rope   -   -   - 1s. 0d.
>
> 1735. Nov. 5. Paid Clark of Market
>   for bull rope   -   - 1s. 6d.
>
> 1737. Oct. 17. For 2 penny cords at
>   bull baitings   -   - 2d.
>
> 1738. Apl. 20. To Thomas Kilham
>   for new bull rope   - 12s. 6d.
>
> 1740. Sep. 20. Paid to Thomas Kilham
>   for cord to tie the
>   bull rope   - 3d.
>
> 1742. July 27. Bull rope   -   -   - 10s. 6d.
>
> 1750. Apl. 21. To new bull rope   - 10s. 0d.
>
> 1752. Nov. 20. To Wm. Demaine for
>   links   -   -   - 4d.
>
> 1758. Nov. 18. Bull rope, 26 lbs. at
>   6d. per lb.   -   - 13s. 0d."

Like most other towns, bulls had to be baited

before their flesh could be exposed for sale as food. The proceedings of the Court Leet contain particulars of fines imposed on butchers for not observing the regulation. Details of three cases are as follow :—

"Oct. 4., 1680.—Presented this day by Robert Goodgion, one of ye jury, that John Mitchell, of Skipton, in sum'r last killed one bull and did not bait him, contrary to ye paine, for which wee fine him according to ye paine.

October 17th, 1739.—Whereas Robert Heelis and Robert Johnson, clerks of the market for the burg of Skipton for the year seventeen hundred and thirty-eight, have presented unto us that Peter Moorby, a butcher within this burg, hath kiled and sold within the burg aforesaid a bull without baiteing, we, the jury, do amerce the sd Moorby for so doing the sum of six shillings and eight pence.

May 5th, 1742.—We, the jurymen, do amerce Samuel Goodgion and Benjamin Shires each the sum of 3s. 4d., for exposeing to sale in the market-place within the manor bull beefe not being baited."

Edwards, in his "Remarkable Charities," a work compiled from the reports made by the Commissioners for enquiring into Charities in England and Wales, gives an instance of money left for purchasing a bull for baiting. "George Staverton," it is stated, "by will, in May, 1661, gave out of his Staines' house a yearly sum of £6 to buy

a bull, which bull he gave to the poor of
Wokingham town and parish, being baited, and
the gift money, hide, and offal to be sold and
bestowed upon the poor children in stockings of
the Welsh and shoes." Until 1823, the baiting
of the animal took place yearly on the 21st
December, in the market-place of Wokingham.
In that year the corporation determined upon dis-
continuing such a proceeding, which has since
accordingly been omitted. At Christmas, 1835,
the mob broke open in the night the place
where one of the animals was kept, and
baited it. Meat to the value of twenty pounds
is distributed amongst the poor of the place,
the property left having increased in value.
Some important particulars of this charity
will be found in Dyer's " British Popular
Customs."

Long before the Act was passed which put an
end to bull-baiting, the more enlightened members
of the community recognised the baneful effects of
the sport, and attempted to stop it. Preston, as
we have previously stated, was a popular place for
the pastime. The corporation, on the 11th
November, 1726, decided that in future no
bull be bought at the charge of the Cor-

poration. The resolution strongly condemned the sport.

In 1802, a bill to abolish bull-baiting was thrown out of the Commons. Mr. Windham made a powerful speech in favour of the custom. The brutal pastime continued down to 1835, when it was made illegal by Act of Parliament.

The Badge of Poverty.

THE noble families of England in the days of old took great pride in their badges. From the time of Edward I. down to the age of Queen Elizabeth badges were in general use. It was regarded as a punishment of the deepest degradation to deprive a gentleman of his badge. It was handed down with pride from sire to son. In Shakespeare's *Henry VI.*, Clifford says :

"Might I but know thee by thy household badge."

In the reign of William III. a badge most distasteful to the poor was introduced. Persons receiving parish relief had to wear on the right shoulder or sleeve a piece of red or blue cloth bearing the letter P and the initial of the parish to which they belonged. For example, Alfreton paupers would have A.P. in letters of metal on a coloured cloth ground. This would enable the thoughtless to sneer at their poverty, perhaps brought about by circumstances over which they had not any control.

Old parish books contain many allusions to the

wearing of badges, or rather the refusal to wear them. We extract from the old vestry book of Burton-on-Trent the following minute, dated September 6th, 1702 : " Whereas several persons that receive alms out of the poore's levy of this liberty do often omitt the wearing of the public badge of this town or observe the same—

" It is therefore ordered that when any such poore person or persons shall, or their children, bee seen without such badge or to observe the same that upon the view of either of the overseers or reliable information thereof to them of the neglect of wearing or observing such badge, such poore person or persons shall for a fortnight thenafter lose his and their allowance out of the poore's levy and the like penalty shall be continued so often as any such offence shall be committed, and not put in pay again till such badge be worn."

We gather from subsequent entries in these records that many refused to obey the order, and caused the town authorities a good deal of trouble. They appear to have dealt with the refractory persons with a firm hand. It is ordered, under date of June 6th, 1703, as follows: " That Elizabeth Salisbury, Mary Budworth, Hannah Scott, and Ann Hinckley be taken out of the

constant pay on their stubborn refusal to wear
the badge publicly."

The poor enjoyed very little peace in this
parish. In the same old book we find an entry
dated December 10th, 1749: "Whereas great
numbers of vagrants and sturdy beggars have
for some time past frequented this town, and for
preventing the same for the future it is ordered
that Robert Hinds be allowed 25s. quarterly for
the care and pains in looking after and driving
out of the town all vagrants and beggars both by
night and day."

The municipal records of Liverpool contain
the following, under date of May 13th, 1685:
"Ordered that all persons whose names are in
the Poore Booke, and who receave almes in this
burrough shall weare a pewter badge wth ye
towne's armes engraved on it, and such as refuse
to weare them are hereby ordered not to have
anie releife from this towne."

About 1775, the parish authorities of Birmingham decided to compel persons receiving
relief to wear badges, and had a number of
badges cast for this purpose. "An old woman,"
says Roberts, in his "Social History," "was the
first brought before the board, who told her what

the order was, and gave her the badge of disgrace. She courtesied, and expressed her readiness to do as they commanded without delay. Pulling up her gown, she pinned it on her petticoat; then letting fall her gown, the badge was invisible, and thus the plan was frustrated, to the great annoyance of the parish law makers."

The enforcement of wearing the badge of poverty was distasteful, more especially amongst women, who appear to have had a greater objection to it than men. Happily, and very properly, it was at a later period abolished by Act of Parliament.

Patents to Wear Nightcaps.

AMONGST curiosities of history may be included patents to wear nightcaps. Several noblemen and gentlemen, chiefly in their old age, have been granted the privilege of appearing at Court and in other places in their caps. Perhaps the most interesting document bearing on this subject is a patent granted by Queen Mary to the Earl of Sussex. He suffered much from colds in his advanced years, and on this account petitioned her Majesty to grant permission for him to wear his nightcap when he waited upon her. The Queen readily granted his request, adding that he might wear two if he wished to do so.

The following is a copy of the patent :

" Know ye, that we do give to our well-beloved and trusty cousin and councillor, Henry, Earl of Sussex, Viscount Fitzwalter, and Lord of Egremond and Pernell, licence and pardon to wear his cap, coif, or nightcap, or any two of them, at his pleasure, as well in our presence as in the

presence of any other person or persons within
this realm, or in any other place within our
dominions wheresoever, during his life ; and these
our letters shall be sufficient warrant in his
behalf."

Miss Agnes Strickland, in her "Lives of the
Queens of England," supposes that the foregoing
is unique ; such, however, is not the fact.   Long
before the reign of Mary, King John had granted
a similar honour to Courcy, Baron of Kinsale in
Ireland.   Christopher Brown, the father of the
celebrated Robert Brown, founder of the Brownists
(a sect better known in later years as Independents),
had a grant whereby he might put on his cap
where he pleased, and only put it off at his own
ease and pleasure.

A patent granted by Henry the Eighth to Walter
Copinger has been preserved, and we are able to
place a copy of it before our readers.   It is as
follows :—

" Henry, by the grace of God, king of England
and France and lord of Ireland, to all men our
own subjects, as well of spiritual pre-eminence
and dignities as of the temporal authority, these our
letters hearing and seeing, and to every of them
greeting.   Whereas we be credibly informed that

our trusty and well-beloved subject, Walter Copinger, is so diseased in his head that without his great danger he cannot be conveniently discovered of the same. In consideration whereof we have by these presents licensed him to use and wear his bonet upon his said head, as well in our presence as elsewhere, at his liberty. Wherefore we will and command you and every of you to permit and suffer him so to do, without any your challenge, disturbance, or interruption to the contrary, as you and every of you tender our pleasure. Given under our signet at our manor of Greenwich the 24th day of October, in the 4th year of your reign, Henry R."

Anent wearing the hat in the presence of the monarch in Russia, we have a good story from Mr. G. A. Sala. "The Czar of Russia in the time of Elizabeth," says Mr. Sala, "once observed Sir Jeremy Bowes, the English ambassador to Moscow, wearing his hat in the Imperial presence. He had already punished one rash person for a similar offence, by ordering his hat to be nailed to his head. 'Have you not heard, sir,' asked the Czar, 'of the person I have punished for such an insult?' 'Yes, sire,' replied Sir Jeremy, 'but I am the Queen of England's ambassador,

who never yet stood bareheaded to any prince
whatever; her I represent, and on her I depend
to do me right if I am insulted.'   'A brave fellow
this,' exclaimed the Czar, addressing one of the
nobles, 'who dares thus act and talk for his
sovereign's honour! Which of you would do so
for me?'"

A Foolish Fashion.

AN absurd fashion of sticking black patches on the face has prevailed in various countries at different periods. The earliest reference we have found occurs in Roman history, from which we gather that it was general amongst women in the closing years of the Empire. The introduction to England was as late as the Elizabethan era, and the first to practice it were the fops of the day, who embellished their faces with patches shaped in the form of stars, crescents, and lozenges. Several of the poets directed their satires against the usage, but with little effect, for it was kept up for a considerable period.

It appears that the man who went a-wooing made a display of patches, for, says Glapthorne, in his "Lady's Privilege," 1640 :—"If it be a lover's part you are to act, take a black spot or two. I can furnish you ; 'twill make your face more amorous, and appear more gracious in your mistress' eyes." Ten years later we find the first mention of English women adopting this fashion. It occurs in a work entitled the "Artificial Changeling," by Bulwer, and bears date of 1653. "Our ladies," says Bulwer, " have lately entertained a vain custom of spotting their faces, out of an affectation of a mole, to set off their beauty, such as Venus had ; and it is well if one black patch will serve to make their faces remarkable, for some fill their visages full of them, varied unto all manner of shapes." He gives with his notice an illustration, which we reproduce. It will be observed that in addition to four stars there is a coach and horses. The latter was a form of the

patch which met with much favour with the ladies. A volume issued in 1658, called " Wit Restored," contains the following allusion to this custom :—

> " Her patches are of every cut,
>   For pimples or for scars ;
>   Here's all the wandering planet's signs,
>   And some of the fixed stars ;
>   Already gummed to make them stick,
>   They need no other sky."

The informing Samuel Pepys, in his

"Diary," has several items on this theme. He wrote, under date November 4th, 1660, thus: " My wife seemed very pretty to-day, it being the first time I had given her leave to wear a black patch." On the 20th of the same month, he says that his wife, with two or three patches on her face, appeared much handsomer than the Princess Henrietta.

In the days of Queen Anne, political dames indicated with patches the party to which they belonged; the Whigs patched the right cheek, the Tories the left, and those that were neutral embellished both cheeks. In the *Spectator* for June 2nd, 1771, is an interesting letter by Addison on this theme. It also states that a lady stipulated, at the signing of the marriage articles, that she should be permitted to patch on which side she pleased, whatever might be her husband's opinions.

A writer in the *World* for the year 1754 speaks of the patch increasing in size as to almost overwhelm the face. Shortly after this the custom appears to have fallen from its high place, and in the course of a few more years to have gone completely out of fashion.

Wedding Notices in the Last Century.

A CURIOUS feature in the marriage announcements of the last century was their giving details respecting the dowry and personal charms of the bride. Our forefathers do not appear to have been backward at making known the fortunes they had obtained with their wives. Matters that we should regard as belonging to ourselves, or at the most to our intimate friends, were given to the world with trumpet-like sound. One can hardly pick up a magazine or newspaper of the period without finding wedding notices similar to the following, which is drawn from the *Gentleman's Magazine* of 1781:—

"Married, the Rev. Mr. Roger Waina, of York, about twenty-six years of age, to a Lincolnshire lady, upwards of eighty, with whom he is to have £8,000 in money, £300 per annum, and a coach-and-four during life only." How long this unequal pair enjoyed matrimonial bliss we are not in a position to state. He certainly

o

got a good fortune with his dame, but one is disposed to think that a union at the price is not to be envied when so many lovely women are prepared to give heart and hand to worthy men, and add poetry to the prose of life.

In the same periodical of March, 1735, we read :—

"John Parry, Esq., of Carmarthenshire, married to a daughter of Walter Lloyd, Esq., member of that county ; a fortune of £8,000."

Another announcement of the same month and year, in the same magazine, says : —

"The Earl of Antrim, of Ireland, to Miss Betty Pennefeather, a celebrated beauty and toast of that kingdom."

It may be inferred that, as a fortune is not mentioned, the noble Earl preferred beauty to money, and that the charms of Miss Pennefeather made amends for the lack of gold.

The following notices are drawn from *Williamson's Liverpool Advertiser* for 1759 : —

"Liverpool, May 25. On Tuesday last was married at Hale, Dr. Zachariah Leafe, of Preccot, to Miss Martha Clough, of Halewood, an agreeable young lady of 18 years of age, with a very genteel fortune."

"July 13. Married on Sunday last, Mr. Edward Bailey to Mrs. Hannah Knight, a widow, with a handsome fortune."

"Sept. 21. On Thursday, 13th inst., at Kendal, in Westmoreland, Colonel George Wilson, to Miss James, of Kirkby Stephen, an agreeable young lady, with a fortune of 14,000 pounds. Last week, at the same place, John Heyes, M.D., to Miss Smyth, an accomplished lady, with a considerable fortune. Also,

"On Sunday last, the 16th instant, Mr. John Cummins, an eminent hosier, to Miss Betty Newby, a genteel lady, with a fortune of £900 (nine hundred pounds)."

"Last week, Mr. Thomas Hodgson, merchant and insurance broker, to Miss Bent, of Warrington, a young lady with a genteel fortune."

"Sept. 28. The paragraph inserted in our last, relative to the pretended marriage of John Heyes, M.D., and Colonel George Wilson, at Kendal, in Westmoreland, is entirely false; and as those gentlemen resent the affront, unless the author of the letter of intelligence sent per post to the publishers of this paper from Kendal, immediately apply to them, their letter and real name shall be exposed publickly."

"November 9. Married, Mr. Richard Walker, merchant, to Miss Watt, sister to Mr. Richard Watt, merchant in Kingston, in Jamaica, a young lady with a genteel fortune, and other accomplishments necessary to render the marriage state happy."

Says the *Newcastle Courant*, of February 11th, 1764 :—"A few days since was married at London, Mr. Joseph Milbourn, of Cockle Park, in Northumberland, gunner on board his Majesty's ship 'Windsor,' to Mrs. Norton, of Gosport, in the Isle of Wight, an agreeable widow lady, with a fortune of £6,000."

The *Leeds Intelligencer*, for July 3, 1764, chronicles :—

"On Thursday last was married Mr. John Wormald, of this town, merchant, to Miss Rebecca Thompson, daughter of the late ——— Thompson, Esq., of Staincliffe Hall, near Batley, an agreeable young lady with a fortune of upwards of £4,000."

In the same journal of the 4th September following, appears the announcement as under :—

"Yesterday morning was married the Rev. Mr. Wilson, vicar of Otley, to Miss Nancy Furness, of the same place, a most agreeable young lady, endowed with all the qualifications necessary to make the marriage state happy."

Respecting wedding dowries, it is said that about the year 1770, a tradesman was residing in London who had disposed of eleven daughters in marriage, and as a fortune for each he had given their weight in halfpence. It is suggested that they were rather bulky, as the lightest of them weighed fifty pounds two shillings and eight-pence.

Towards the close of the century, the announce-ments of marriages were somewhat toned down, as the following, culled from the newspapers, show. One dated January 5th, 1789, states :—

" Sunday se'nnight, at St. Aulkman's Church, Shrewsbury, A. Holbecke, Esq., of Slowley Hill, near Coleshill, in this country, to Mrs. Ashby, of Shrewsbury, a very agreeable lady, with a good fortune."

In a paper dated for January 2nd, 1792, we read :—

" Yesterday, at St. Martin's Church, William Lucas, Esq., of Holywell, in Northamptonshire, to Miss Legge, only daughter of the late Mr. Francis Legge, builder, of this town ; an agreeable young lady, with a handsome fortune."

On 29th October, 1798, we find an account of the marriage of "an agreeable lady with a genteel fortune." And in April, 1783, we find it stated that the marriage of Mr. George Donisthorpe to "the agreeable Mrs. Mary Barker" took place; but there is not any mention of money. We believe that the following is one of the latest instances of this kind of announcement. It appeared in *Aris's Birmingham Gazette* for July 14th, 1800, and records the marriage of the Right Hon. Mr. Canning, Under-Secretary of State, to Miss Scott, sister to the Marchioness of Titchfield, " with £100,000 fortune."

Selling Wives.

IT was generally believed in bygone days that in this country a husband might lawfully sell his wife to another man, provided he conducted the transaction in some public place and delivered her to the purchaser with a halter about her neck. The sales were duly reported in the newspapers of the period, without any special comment, as items of every-day news. In some instances market tolls were collected similar to those charged for animals brought to the public market.

An examination of a number of old journals, magazines, date-books, and other publications, has enabled us to bring together the following authenticated cases of men selling their wives :— Says the *Ipswich Journal*, January 28, 1787 : "A farmer of the parish of Stowupland sold his wife to a neighbour for five guineas, and, being happy to think he had made a good bargain, presented her with a guinea to buy a new gown. He then went to Stowmarket and gave orders for the bells to be rung on the occasion." Formerly the church bells were set a-ringing to celebrate a variety of events. Merry peals were rung when news arrived of victories in the field of battle, and frequently owners of racehorses would cause the bells to be rung in honour of their horses winning important races.

In the *Times* of March 30th, 1796, it is stated that at Sheffield a person named Lees sold his wife for the small sum of sixpence to a man called Hall. The woman was delivered to her purchaser with a halter round her neck. Her husband gave a guinea to have her taken next day to Manchester by coach. The paragraph is thus concluded : " It would be well if some law was enforced to put a stop to such degrading traffic."

We read in the *Times* of July 18th, 1797, that " on Friday a butcher exposed his wife for sale in Smithfield Market, near the Ram Inn, with a halter about her neck, and one about her waist, which tied her to a railing, when a hog-driver was the happy purchaser, who gave the husband three guineas and a crown for his departed rib. Pity it is there is no stop put to such depraved conduct in the lower order of people." On the following day it is stated, " By some mistake in our report of the Smithfield Market, we had not learned the

average price of wives for the last week." The
writer further says : " The increasing value of the
fair sex is esteemed by several eminent writers as
a certain criterion of increasing civilization.
Smithfield has, on this ground, strong pretentions
to refined improvement, as the price of wives has
risen in that market from half-a-guinea to three
guineas and a half."

The next item, from the *Times* of September
19th, 1797, is somewhat jocular in style: "An
hostler's wife in the country lately fetched twenty-
five guineas. We hear there is to be a sale of
wives soon at Christie's. We have no doubt they
will soon go off well." In the same journal for
December 2nd, 1797, it is recorded that, "at the
last sale of wives there was but a poor show,
though there were plenty of bidders. One alone
went off well, being bought by a Taylor, who
outbid eight of his competitors."

A wife and child, with a quantity of furniture,
were sold in 1802 at the Market Cross, Chapel-
en-le-Frith, Derbyshire, for eleven shillings. The
sale is reported in the *Morning Herald*, and it is
there stated that there was "as much furniture as
would set up a beggar." In the same year a
butcher sold his wife by public auction in the

Hereford market. The lot realised one pound four shillings and a bowl of punch.

Here are particulars of another wife sale at Sheffield, drawn from the *Doncaster Gazette* of March 25th, 1803 :—" A fellow sold his wife as a cow in Sheffield market-place a few days ago. The lady was put into the hands of a butcher, who held her by a halter fastened round her waist. ' What do you ask for your cow ?' said a bystander. ' A guinea,' replied the husband. ' Done !' cried the other, and immediately led away his bargain. We understand that the purchaser and his ' cow ' live very happily together."

Particulars of a sale of a wife in Hull on February 14th, 1806, are given in the " Annual Register " and in the local newspapers. They are as follow :—" A man named John Gosthorpe, of Patrington, exposed his wife for sale in the market at Hull about one o'clock ; but owing to the crowd which such an extraordinary occurrence had gathered together, he was obliged to defer the sale and take her away. About four o'clock, however, he again brought her out, and she was sold for twenty guineas, and delivered, in a halter, to a person named Houseman, who had lodged with them four or five years." A local journal of the period, referring to this matter, says :—" From their frequency of late years, the common people have imbibed an opinion that the proceedings are strictly legal, and binding by law."

At Knaresborough, Yorkshire, in 1807, a man sold his wife "in the usual style" at the Market Cross for sixpence and a quid of tobacco. The *Morning Post*, in reporting this case, refers to it as "one of those disgraceful scenes which have of late become too common."

In the year 1820 a man called Brouchet, residing at the village of Broughton, led his wife to the cattle market at Canterbury, and requested a cattle salesman to sell her for him. He declined, saying that he sold cattle and not women. Brouchet next hired a cattle-pen, for which he paid sixpence, the amount usually charged for tollage. He led his wife into it by a halter, and soon disposed of her for five shillings to a resident in the city.

At Carlisle, on the 7th of April, 1832, the sale of a woman brought together a great number of people. The event was announced by the bell-man, and at noon, Joseph Thomson, a farmer, who had been married for three years, placed his wife in a chair, with a halter round her neck.

He delivered the following amusing address :—
" Gentlemen, I have to offer to your notice my
wife, Mary Anne Thomson, otherwise Williams,
whom I mean to sell to the highest and fairest
bidder. Gentlemen, it is her wish as well as mine
to part for ever. She has been to me only a born
serpent. I took her for my comfort and the good
of my home ; but she became my tormentor, a
domestic curse, a night invasion, and a daily plague.

" Gentleman, I speak truth from my heart when
I beg that we may be delivered from troublesome
wives and frolicsome women ! Avoid them as
you would a mad dog, a roaring lion, a loaded
pistol, cholera morbus, Mount Etna, or any other
pestilential thing in nature.

" Now I have shown you the dark side of my
wife, and told you her faults and failings, I will
introduce the bright and sunny side of her, and
explain her qualifications and goodness.

" She can read novels and milk cows ; she can
laugh and weep with the same ease that you
could take a glass of ale when thirsty. Indeed,
gentlemen, she reminds me of what the poet says
of women in general :—

> ' Heaven gave to women the peculiar grace
> To laugh, to weep, to cheat the human race.'

She can make butter and scold the maid ; she can sing Moore's melodies and plait her frills and caps ; she cannot make rum, gin, or whiskey, but she is a good judge of the quality, from long experience in tasting them. I therefore offer her with all her perfections and imperfections for the sum of fifty shillings."

No one seemed in a hurry to purchase Mrs. Thomson, and the seller had to wait about an hour for a customer. Eventually, a man named Henry Mears bought her for twenty shillings and a Newfoundland dog. The report of the proceedings concludes by stating that "they parted in perfect good temper—Mears and the woman going one way, Thomson and the dog another."

An important note bearing on this theme is given in Chambers's " Book of Days." A case, it is stated, " occurred in 1835, in which a woman was sold by her husband for fifteen pounds ; she at once went home with the buyer ; she survived both buyer and seller, and then married again. Some property came to her in the course of years from her first husband, for, notwithstanding claims put forth by other relatives, she was able to maintain in a court of law that the sale did not and could not vitiate her rights as his widow."

At the West Riding sessions, in 1837, a man was tried for selling, or trying to sell, his wife, and committed to prison for two months with hard labour. The case excited much surprise and interest at the time.

Nottingham supplies two cases. According to the " Nottingham Date-Book," on the 28th April, 1852, " About twelve o'clock a female, about thirty-eight years of age, accompanied by her husband and two of his companions, stood in the market place, near the sheep pens. The female was the wife of Edward Stevenson, and he had come to the determination, with her consent, to dispose of her by auction. A new rope, value sixpence, was around her neck. Stevenson, with his wife standing unabashed by his side, held the rope and exclaimed :—

" ' Here is my wife for sale. I shall put her up at two shillings and sixpence.'

" A man named John Burrows, apparently a navvy, proffered a shilling for the lot, and after some haggling, she was knocked off at this price, and they all went to the Spread Eagle to sign articles of agreement, the lady being the only party able to sign her name."

Coming down to the present time, we find, in 1882, at Alfreton, Derbyshire, a husband sold his wife in a public-house for a glass of beer.

The latest instance of a wife being sold of which we have particulars, was brought to light in the Sheffield County Court, on the 13th July, 1887. A man named Hall admitted that some time ago he bought another man's wife for five shillings. An agreement was drawn up at the time of the sale, which read as follows :—

"At the Royal Oak, Sheffield, I, Abraham Boothroyd, agree to sell my wife Clara to William Hall, both of Sheffield, for the sum of 5s." The document was signed by Boothroyd and Hall, and witnessed by two other men.

The Story of the Tinder=box.

UP to the third decade of this century all throughout the land, in some secluded places for many years later, the friction match had not yet appeared, and those who wished to enlighten their darkness had to do it by flint and steel. On every cottage mantelshelf stood, as one of the essentials of home life, the tinder-box and its accompaniments. A specimen of this old-fashioned domestic appliance is before us as we write, and of a pattern that was to be found with curious uniformity of form and fashion in almost every house in the country. It is not to be styled a thing of beauty, and in general its appearance is commonplace, in which it differs from many other adjuncts of old cottage life.

The tinder-box before us is of tin, circular in form, four inches in diameter, and one-and-a-half in height. It has a lid which fits over it canister-wise, and in the centre of the lid is soldered a tin tube of over an inch in length, to be used as a candlestick. The box has a small handle at the side. The tinder, which consisted simply of burnt linen, lay flat at the bottom of the box, and a disc of tin, with handle at the top, was used to extinguish the sparks when they had served their purpose. This disc is called the damper. The flint and steel usually lay in the box above the damper. The flint was generally the nearest

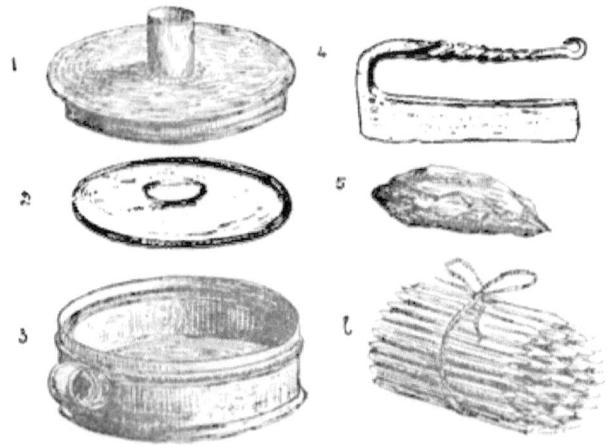

1. LID WITH SOCKET FOR CANDLE. 2. DAMPER. 3. TINDER-BOX. 4. STEEL "STRIKE-A-LIGHT." 5. FLINT. 6. MATCHES.

piece that offered itself; occasionally a pre-historic weapon-head has been found to be used, or a large flake, but the best and quickest ignitory results were met with by using a flint nodule. The steel or striker is made from an old file bent into a U shape. In addition to the above articles, it was necessary to have matches, which were made of red or white deal dipped in sulphur.

P

The *modus operandi* of striking a light in those
dark days is exemplified by the sketch of a girl of
the last century thus engaged.   Removing the
candlestick lid, and taking out of the box all but

STRIKING A LIGHT.

the tinder, she holds the flint firmly in the left
hand, and with the steel held perpendicularly in
the right hand, strikes forcibly downwards, the
edge of the steel, about an eighth of an inch in

breadth, passing vertically along any convenient facet of the stationary flint. With each blow, if adroitly directed, a number of sparks will fly in all directions, though naturally downwards. One of these, sooner or later, alights on a sensitive portion of the tinder, and transmits its fire. The tinder spark, either fanned by the breath, or left to the combustibility of the substance, flits about on the charred linen rag, and the girl has now to apply to it the point of a sulphur match. It ignites, bursts into a blue blaze, and the thing is done; the candle is lighted, and the fires, candles, or lamps were assured a light. Some persons used the steel as the anvil, striking it with the flint, but most employed it as above described.

The matches were either made by the con- sumers themselves, —sometimes by their children, —or purchased from gipsies who included these among their many useful manufactures. They were sold at the beginning of this century at the rate of five bundles for a penny : they were pointed and dipped in sulphur at both ends.

The Invention of Friction Matches.

WHEN the first friction match broke into light, and to whom the credit of its invention ought to be given is a disputed point. The claims of John Walker and Isaac Holden have been made and maintained in the columns of newspapers and the pages of books of reference. It will not be without interest and importance to examine the statements adduced on behalf of each.

John Walker for many years carried on business as an apothecary in a humble way in High Street, Stockton-on-Tees. He died on May 1st, 1859, aged seventy-eight years. Alderman Richard Jackson, of Stockton-on-Tees, enjoyed the friendship of Mr. Walker, and was ever ready to advocate his claims as the inventor of the lucifer match. Writing in the columns of the *Northern Echo*, under date of May 6th, 1871, Mr. Jackson gave some interesting information on this subject, and well worthy of being reproduced. "I have not the slightest doubt," said

Mr. Jackson, "that the invention of lucifer matches is due to our late fellow-townsman, Mr. John Walker, chemist and druggist, who had for his place of business the shop No. 59, High Street, Stockton. I knew Mr. Walker personally and intimately, and have had many a friendly chat with him both on this subject and others. In the year 1860, I sent a communication to the *Illustrated London News,* in consequence of an article in that journal with the heading, 'The Origin or Invention of Lucifer Matches.' After alluding to the tinder-box and phosphorus match-boxes, it is stated, 'Suddenly and successfully, but where we have not been able to learn, the lucifer matches invaded the province of the old tar matches.' Before replying to the article in the *Illustrated London News,* I communicated with an old friend, the editor of a local newspaper, who confirmed my conviction that the world at large is indebted to Mr. John Walker for this very useful invention. I may say that Mr. Walker was frequently and urgently pressed by his numerous friends to take out a patent, but he always declined, saying it was not worth while doing so, considering the simple and trifling nature of the article. Mr. Walker died in

Stockton in the year 1859. The facts as stated
in the local paper to which I refer were published
in 1852, and were as follow:—Mr. Walker was
preparing some lighting mixture for his own use,
when a match, after being dipped in the preparation, took fire by accidental friction upon the
hearth. This was the first friction match, and the
hint was not lost. He commenced making
friction matches, selling with each box a piece of
doubled sand paper to set them in flames by
pressure of the thumb and a sharp pull. It was
in the month of August, 1827, that he began the
sale, and his first customer was the late Mr. John
Hixon, solicitor, of Stockton. Harrison Burn
was employed to make the matches, and the
boxes were made by Mr. John Ellis, at three-half-
pence each, the price of a box containing fifty
being one shilling. I think, after perusing the
above, you will have no doubt that Mr. Walker is
really the inventor of this useful and now indis-
pensable article. I have always endeavoured, in
various parts of the Continent, as well as in
England, to establish these facts, that justice may
be done to the departed." The foregoing clearly
places Mr. Walker's claims on record, and it only
remains for us to state that the local historical

works, including the "Annals of Stockton,"
compiled by Henry Heavisides, and published in
1865, credit Walker with the invention.

In recent years the claims of Mr. Isaac
Holden have been more widely known. His life
reads like a romance, and forms a charming
chapter in "Fortunes Made in Business." The
story of his career does not come within the scope
of this chapter ; a few biographical facts must, however, be given. He was born on the 7th of May,
1807, at Harlet, a village situated between Paisley
and Glasgow. His father was a native of
Cumberland, and there followed the occupation of
small farmer and lead miner. Subsequently
Holden obtained a situation as headsman at
Wellington pit, Nitshill, and he was thus
employed when his son Isaac, named after himself,
was born. He gave his son a good education, and
after some changes young Holden was engaged as
classical master at Castle Street Academy,
Reading. He there gave a series of lectures
on chemistry and other subjects, and it was at
one of these, in October, 1829, that Mr. Holden
brought into notice his match. The story of his
discovery he related to a Select Committee of the
House of Commons appointed to enquire into the

working of the patent laws. "I began as an inventor on a very small scale," said Mr. Holden to the committee. "For what I know, I was the first inventor of lucifer matches; but it was the result of a happy thought. In the morning I used to get up at four o'clock in order to pursue my studies, and I used at that time the flint and steel, in the use of which I found very great inconvenience. I gave lectures in chemistry at the time at a very large academy. Of course I knew, as other chemists did, the explosive material that was necessary in order to produce instantaneous light; but it was very difficult to obtain a light on wood by that explosive material, and the idea occurred to me to put under the explosive mixture sulphur. I did that, and published it in my next lecture, and showed it. There was a young man in the room whose father was a chemist in London, and he immediately wrote to his father about it, and shortly afterwards lucifer matches were issued to the world. I believe that was the first occasion that we had the present lucifer match, and it was one of those inventions that some people think ought not to be protected by a patent. I think that if all inventions were like that, or if we could distinguish one from the other, the principle might hold good. If all inventions were ascertained and carried out into practice with as much facility as in this case, no one would perhaps think of taking out a patent. I was urged to go and take out a patent immediately ; but I thought it was so small a matter, and it cost me so little labour, that I did not think it proper to go and get a patent, otherwise I have no doubt it would have been very profitable." It will be observed from Mr. Jackson's letter that Mr. Walker was the first in the field with the friction match. Mr. Holden has made a great reputation as an inventor, manufacturer, and a large-hearted man, ever ready to assist in the furtherance of religious, charitable, and political objects.

The prejudice against the lucifer match at first was very great, and it was by no means confined to the ignorant members of the community. Respecting old-time objects we have heard some good stories. One of the best is related by Mr. Robert Gibbs, F.S.A., of Aylesbury. "When a schoolboy," Mr. Gibbs tells us, "one of my fellows left Aylesbury to reside in London ; after an absence of some months he returned, and like the monkey that had seen the world he was

extremely loquacious, and related with great glee
to his old companions what sights he had seen in
London. He had been to the top of St. Paul's
and to the bottom of the Thames Tunnel; had
seen the waxworks, and also Mazeppa at the play;
knew the height of Gog and Magog; indeed,
according to his description, he knew as much
about London as though he had laid every brick
in it. At this period very few Aylesbury boys
had seen the great city, there being no railways,
no excursion trains or half-tickets, and forty miles
was too long to walk, so we were glad to hear
something about a place in which we felt such
a great interest. Living in a comparatively small
town, our ideas were proportionately contracted;
we thought our Free School room so large that a
larger erection would be a dangerous building:
that our church was a model; and our County
Hall could not be exceeded as a grand building
all over London. Our Cockney friend, however,
took some of the conceit out of us when he told
us that our schoolroom was not so big as the
Mansion House coal-hole; that our church would
stand in one of the corners of St. Paul's, and that
Day and Martin's blacking shop was as large
as our County Hall. We knew our old friend's

proclivities, and so deducted a large discount off
the descriptions he gave us of what he had seen in
London.

He, however, played off a joke on us, that at
least caused us all a great surprise. Standing one
day near a building where we had met him, he turned
his face towards the wall to keep off the wind ; he
then put something into his mouth, and on with-
drawing it in less than a moment, produced a
flaming match. We all thought that our friend
had been taking lessons in necromancy, or had
had dealings with the Evil One, as we could not
account otherwise for the instantaneous production
of the light. 'There,' said he, exhibiting a flaming match, 'you've nothing of this kind here at
Aylesbury. It is a new match now to be had in
London, and is called a lucifer.' He then produced a very small box containing a few more, on
which he had expended sixpence. He gave me
one as a special favour, and this was my first
introduction to lucifer matches.

Our Cockney friend must have been an early
bird in obtaining a lucifer at this period, which, if
I make no mistake, was about 1829. I heard
nothing more of lucifers for some years after. I
took the marvellous match home to my mother,

and struck it against the chimney piece, when, to her surprise, it gave out a brilliant flame. 'Now,' I said, 'you may throw away your tinder-box, for these new-fashioned matches are to be had in London.' 'No,' said she, 'no such things about my house. Matches which light themselves will find no place here. Why, we should some night be all burnt to death in our beds! Give me my old-fashioned tinder-box!'"

Many old folk in America objected to the friction match, regarding it as a dangerous article. Mr. Henry M. Brooks, the author of several works relating to the olden time, has drawn from a Salem newspaper, of June 30th, 1836, the following paragraph:—" Notwithstanding the convenience of those dangerous little articles, which are in almost everybody's hands, but which with all their charms bid fair to prove a heavy curse to the community, we learn that there is one man in Salem, a respectable tradesman, who keeps a store where we should generally expect to find such things, but who has never sold them, nor allowed them to be used on his premises. At his house and shop he sticks to the old-fashioned flint, steel, and tinder. He shows his wisdom in so doing. How many more can say as much?"

Body Snatching.

THE nefarious operations of the body snatchers form a startling chapter in the history of civilization. For an extended period down to the year 1832, when an alteration was made in the laws of England, anatomical teachers mainly relied on the odious fraternity of resurrection-men for obtaining subjects for dissection.

We have conversed with several men who have watched churchyards to guard the graves of the recently buried dead. An old friend informed us that in the year 1828 he watched Drypool churchyard for fourteen nights in the company of a friend, to prevent the grave of a relative being opened. On four or five subsequent occasions he performed for other people the same office. We have next to state, on authority that cannot be gainsaid, that the grave of an infant was opened and the body taken from the same churchyard about this period. It was discovered under painful circumstances. The father lost a second child, and wished it to be interred in the same grave as the one he had previously buried. He waited upon the grave-digger and made his desire known. The sexton pointed out another part of the burial ground as the resting-place of the first child, but where the parent knew he had not laid his infant. That proceeding of course led to the suspicion that foul play had been used, and he caused the grave to be opened in which he knew his child had been buried, and much to his grief he found the body had been stolen and only part of the coffin remained. A meeting of the parishioners was called, and it was resolved to enclose the churchyard by a high wall. It occurred, however, to the worthy Vicar, the Rev. Henry Venn, that the proposed wall would shield the body snatchers from the gaze of anyone passing the churchyard, instead of being a protection. Upon his suggestion it was decided to erect a low wall and place on it palisades, so that anyone going to the Garrison might see into the churchyard, and thus prevent the operations of the Resurrectionists. We may add that the graveyard was at that time planted with trees, which now ornament the ground.

In the life of a well-known Hull character, General Jarvis, a good story is told respecting an

incident occurring in Drypool Churchyard, in which
figured the sexton to whom we have adverted.
" I recollect one night," says the " General," " I
was preparing to sleep under the lee of a stack of
straw in Drypool, when it came on to snow very
heavily. I therefore took up a good armful of
straw and ran into Drypool Churchyard, where
I knew of a vault having a hole broken
in one end. I popped in my straw, and then
popped in myself, and then slept very soundly till
broad daylight, when I was awakened by the
grave-digger swinging his arms to and fro,
and striking each hand against the opposite
shoulder, for the purpose of warming his benumbed
digits. After employing himself thus for a few
minutes, he rested on his spade, and made the
following sensible soliloquy :—" I wish to heaven
people would contrive to die in warmer weather ;
it's starvation work for the gravedigger.' I put
out my head and interrupted him by exclaiming,
in a deep hollow tone of voice, ' What's that you
say, Mr. W-——t ?' Down dropped the spade,
off went his hat, and away he ran as nimble as
a two-year old, over graves and gravestones, as
fast as his legs could carry him ; bolting over the
churchyard wall, and never once looking behind,

until he had safely ensconced himself in the kitchen of the canteen at the Citadel. I followed him at my leisure, and found the worthy sexton, partly recovered from his fright, relating his wonderful ghost story to the astonished maids, when I popped my head over the longsettle just above him, and in the same tone exclaimed as before, 'What's that you say, Mr. W——t?' At the fearful sound he started in terror to his feet, his hair stood on end, his knees trembled under him, and he cried out, 'Oh, Lord! oh, Lord! it's there again.' Thinking I had now pursued the joke far enough, I went round and explained the affair, but it was sometime before poor W—— t could be convinced."

Cases of body snatching appear to have been very common in Hull. In 1832, a body was found in a gig in Charles Street. We have also heard of the head of a man being found in a tavern on Church-side. We have conversed with persons who were engaged to watch the old burial ground in Castle Street. We know a gentleman who watched the grave of a relative in Hessle churchyard some fourteen days, and another who watched the churchyard at Cottingham. Numerous other cases have come under our notice in Hull and neighbourhood.

The history of Rothwell, a village near Leeds, supplies some interesting items. "In 1831," says Mr. John Batty, the local historian, "the Resurrectionists were plying their nefarious trade, and body snatching was a terror to the people. An instance occurred at Ardsley about this date. Several other graveyards were disturbed, but no bodies extracted. A 'Grave Club' was formed at Rothwell, with the object of guarding at night a recent grave for five weeks, until the body had become decomposed. The club became the nucleus of our present 'Dead Brief,' and insisted at the time upon a twelve feet grave, so as to make abstraction of the corpse difficult."

Mr. John Gibbs, F.S.A., of Aylesbury, kindly places at our disposal valuable notes relating to this subject connected with Buckinghamshire. "At the Bucks. Epiphany Sessions, in 1821," says Mr. Gibbs, "three men were tried at Aylesbury and convicted of stealing a body from Great Missenden Churchyard. When these fellows were taken into custody their cart was searched, and another corpse was found and

Q

identified as having been stolen out of
Wendover Churchyard. The prisoners were
sentenced each to a year's imprisonment and a
fine of £10.

"An old man who once worked for me," Mr.
Gibbs tells us, "previously had the care of one of
the road waggons which traversed weekly between
Aylesbury and London ; he told me that on one
occasion a stranger overtook him on the road and
gave him a rough-looking case, which he informed
him would soon be applied for. The case appeared
to have been hurriedly packed, and the waggoner
proceeded to tie it up more securely, when the lid
slipped off, and to his surprise out fell a human
body. He felt inclined to throw the package out
on the roadside, but upon consulting his 'pall'
they thought it better to give information to the
first patrol they met. After travelling some miles,
and before they met with a patrol, a fellow drove
up and applied for the case. ' I was,' said the old
man, 'only too glad to get rid of it, and I gave
the applicant the rough side of my tongue, request-
ing him to transfer his patronage elsewhere ; he
laughed at me for being an old fool, and troubling
myself about what did not concern me, and giving
me what I supposed a sixpence, off he went ; to

my surprise the sixpence turned out to be a half-sovereign.'"

A correspondent, writing in 1879, in the columns of the *British Medical Journal*, gives some strange experiences of his life as a medical student in Dublin. He took part in numerous body-snatching expeditions. "On the first occasion of my joining a night excursion," he says, "an incident occurred sufficient to awaken in me at least momentary alarm. My lot fell to opening a grave in which the interment of a poor woman had taken place. I worked vigorously, and on reaching the frail coffin had no difficulty in breaking back its upper third; but, in stooping down in the usual way, with my head downwards and my feet slanting upwards, I had to support myself by resting my hands on the chest of the dead; when what was my horror to hear a loud prolonged groan from the corpse. I suddenly drew myself upwards, but there was no repetition until I again supported myself with my hands resting on the chest, when another prolonged groan was audible. The cause, on a little examination, became then explicable. The body was an impoverished weakly skeleton, and the pressure of my weight forced the air in the chest up through the trachea and larynx, and produced the sounds which had momentarily terrified me."

Samuel Warren, in his popular work "The Diary of a Late Physician," gives an account of the manner in which the body snatcher opened a grave. His statements, however, are incorrect. We learn from the "Life of Sir Astley Cooper" that the Resurrectionists in exhuming a body did not proceed, as was generally supposed, to remove all the earth with which the grave had been recently filled, and having at length arrived at the coffin, to force off the lid with proper implements, and so remove the body. "This mode of procedure," says Cooper, "would necessarily have occupied a considerable space of time, and rendered the body snatchers proportionately more liable to detection.

"Usually, therefore, to avoid this, they only cleared away the earth above the head of the coffin, taking care to leave that which covered the other portions as far as possible undisturbed. As soon as about one-third of the coffin was thus exposed, they forced a very strong crow-bar, made of a peculiar form for the purpose, into the crevice between the extreme body of the coffin and the lid, which latter, by using the lever as one of the first order, they generally pressed up without much difficulty. It usually happened, at this stage of the proceedings, that the superincumbent weight of the earth on the other portion of the coffin-lid caused it to be snapped across at a distance of about one-third of its length from the fulcrum of the lever. As soon as this had taken place, the body was drawn out, the death gear removed from it and replaced in the coffin, and, finally, the body tied up and placed in its receptacle to be conveyed to its destination. There was seldom any difficulty in extricating a body by these means, unless the lid happened to be sufficiently strong to resist the force of the lever ; this, however, scarcely ever occurred in the coffins of the poorer classes, to which the operations of the Resurrectionists were usually directed."

Cooper tells us " The Resurrection-men were occasionally employed on expeditions into the country to obtain possession of the bodies of those who had been subjected to some important operation, and of which a *post mortem* examination was of the greatest interest to science. Scarcely any distance from London was considered as an insuperable difficulty in the attaining of this object, and as certainly as the Resurrectionist undertook the task, so certain was he of completing it. This was usually an expensive undertaking, but still it did not restrain the most zealous in their profession from occasionally engaging these men in this employment. Sir Astley Cooper, as may be surmised from a consideration of his character, was not backward in availing himself of these opportunities. Nor had he by these means the satisfaction only of deriving information from the examination of these cases, but he was thus enabled to add to his museum many rare records of the triumphs of surgery, and examples of the compensating powers of nature after removal of some important parts of her constitution." We are told that he would "send one of these men considerably more than a hundred miles to obtain a subject, for the purpose of examining the effect of an operation performed years previously, actuated by the desire of acquiring a knowledge of any new facts which the inspection might afford, and of thus being enabled to improve any future operations of the same kind which he might be required to perform."

"The following is a bill on account of one of these expeditions :

1820, June 1st.—Paid Hollis and Vaughan for getting a subject from ——, in the county of ——, a man that Sir Astley Cooper performed an operation upon twenty-four years ago—

Coach for two there and back	£3	12	0
Guards and coachman	0	6	0
Expenses for two days	1	14	6
Carriage of subject, and porter	0	12	6
Subject	7	7	0
	£13	12	0

"A surgeon residing at or near the neighbourhood from which this subject was obtained, had watched the case there for years, and on the death taking place immediately wrote to Sir Astley. Sir Astley, on learning this event, sent for the person from whom I have obtained the above account, and desired him to make an arrangement with the above-named men to obtain the subject, his concluding remark being, 'cost what it may.'"

In the "Life of Sir Astley Cooper" it is stated that "When the regular Resurrectionists had 'got into trouble,' especially if they were active and useful men, and there was nothing very flagrant in the case, the surgeons made great exertions in their favour, and often advanced large sums of money to keep them out of gaol, or to supply their necessities during imprisonment. Sir Astley

Cooper has expended hundreds of pounds for this purpose; nor did the expense rest here, for during the confinement of the husbands the support of their wives and families was a further tax upon him. The first three items in the following bill, which is copied from an account in my possession, will give some idea of the usual rate of these payments :—

1828.	£	s.	d.
Jan. 29. Paid Mr. ——, to pay Mr. —— half the expenses for bailing Vaughan from Yarmouth, and going down	14	7	0
May 6. Paid Vaughan's wife	0	6	0
May 29. Ditto Vaughan, for 26 weeks' confinement, at 10s. per week	13	0	0
Four subjects, two male and two female (Murphy), at twelve guineas each	50	8	0
June 18. Paid Murphy, Wildes, and Naples, finishing money	6	6	0

Occasionally, the sums expended by surgeons on behalf of these men were much larger than the amount mentioned in the above bill. When I was first appointed to the anatomical chair at Guy's Hospital, Murphy had been placed in confinement on account of some disturbances he had been committing in the churchyard at Yarmouth ; a professional friend of mine went down to liberate him, and the amount of his expenditure on this occasion was £160. Another friend of mine, an anatomical teacher, incurred an expense of £50, being the amount of a weekly allowance, continued for two years, to one of the Resurrectionists who was confined in prison."

It is stated the term "finishing money" alludes to a sum of money which was usually given at the end of a session; the amount was generally regulated by the services which had been performed by the Resurrectionist during the time.

In respect to the power of the Resurrectionists, we are told by Mr. Bransby Blake Cooper that Sir Astley Cooper by their aid offered to procure, within three days, the body of a dignified official personage, who had been buried in a place apparently of impenetrable security. The writer goes on to say he had every reason to believe that had he chosen he could have effected this object. Sir Astley Cooper, indeed, stated as much before a committee of the House of Commons, in reply to the following question :—

" Does the state of the law actually prevent the teachers of anatomy from obtaining the body of any person which, in consequence of some peculiarity of structure, they may be particularly desirous of procuring ?"

Sir Astley Cooper replied : " The law does not prevent our obtaining the body of an individual if we think proper ; for there is no person, let his situation in life be what it may, whom, if I were disposed to dissect, I could not obtain."

In answer to another question he said : " The law only enhances the price, and does not prevent the exhumation ; nobody is secured by the law ; it only adds to the price of the subject."

It appears the high prices obtained by the Resurrectionist for subjects often led people, while alive, to try and arrange to obtain money from surgeons on condition that after death their bodies might be dissected. Doctors did not, however, accept the proposals, for as Mr. Cooper naively observes, the agreement could not be enforced, the law not recognising any right of property in a dead body. Sir Astley Cooper declined such offers.

The following letter was addressed to Sir Astley :

" Sir,—I have been informed you are in the habit of purchasing bodys, and allowing the person a sum weekly ; knowing a poor woman that is desirous of doing so, I have taken the liberty of calling to know the truth.

" I remain your humble servant,

"   .   .   ."

He replied briefly thus :—

" The truth is that you deserve to be hanged for making such an unfeeling offer.   A.C."

Among Sir Astley's papers was found written in a fair legible hand, and signed " William Williams," a lengthy document containing a bequest of his body.   We quote part of it as follows :—

" Sir,—Being fully sensible of the uncertainty of this life, and of the mortality of my animated frame—the tabernacle of my soul and of the living spirit that pervades it—and my mind being impressed with the subject of the public benefit to be derived from anatomy, I beg, sir, to communicate to you in writing, what in substance has already been submitted by personal communication to your notice, in regard to my body, graciously bestowed on me by my Maker, when the hereafter desertion of that body by its animated tenants of spirit and soul shall take place.

" If, sir, in your lifetime, I die a bachelor, or unmarried within the Metropolis of Great Britain, called London, or within a convenient distance of the same, or whatever you may consider a convenient distance, I beg, with a view to the furtherance of useful knowledge in the science of anatomy," etc.

We are told the substance of the remainder of this eccentric epistle is simply that if Mr. Williams dies under the above circumstances, his body is to be dissected by or under the supervision of Sir Astley; but that if he should leave a wife, this bequest should be subject to her pleasure and discretion.

Christmas under the Commonwealth.

FOR a long time prior to the period of the Puritans, Christmas was a merry time for rich and poor, and on every hand revelry was the order of the day. English life under the Stuarts became demoralised, the Court setting a baneful example, which the people were not slow to follow. Licentiousness and blasphemy were mistaken for signs of gentility, and little regard was paid to virtue. Debauchery was general, and at the festive seasons was carried to an alarming extent. The Puritans, with all their faults, and it must be admitted that their faults were many, had a regard for sound Christian principles ; and to them the prevailing lack of reverence for virtue, morality, and piety was most distasteful, and caused them to try to put an end to the follies and vices of the age.

King Charles's life was about to close in a tragic manner, at the hands of the headsman, on a scaffold to be erected before the windows of the Palace of Whitehall. The members of the Long Parliament were in power. Old times were changed; the celebration of ancient holidays was forbidden, and in their stead the last Wednesday in each month was to be observed as a solemn fast. Christmas Day in 1644 occurred on the last Wednesday in the year, a circumstance of which the Assembly of Divines took the opportunity of reminding Parliament that the day might be kept "as it ought to be." In compliance with this request, an ordinance was issued directing that Christmas Day should be observed as a fast. This was not altogether according to the ideas of Cromwell; but as the head of a party he had to take cognisance of the opinions of his supporters, and fall in with their behests. The people received the intimation with marked disapproval. To have fasting instead of feasting was a state of things not to be tolerated, and loud and long were the cries against what was deemed an infringe-ment of their ancient rights. In nearly all parts of the country the proclamation was resented, and not a few riots occurred. During this era many were the fruitless attempts to put down this great holiday.

The members of Parliament sat on Christmas Day to transact the business of state, and set an example of work which few felt disposed to follow. The Government ordained that shops were to be opened and markets held, and the work-a-day world to proceed with its usual avocations. The people refused, however, to conduct trade, and in not a few instances broke the windows of those who attempted to dispose of their wares at the holiday season. The aid of the militia had to be sought to maintain order.

At Canterbury on one occasion a serious disturbance occurred. Those in authority directed the holding of a market on Christmas Day, and some dozen shopkeepers opened their premises. The populace, supported by some of the "classes," requested the tradesmen to close their establishments, and on their refusing, broke the windows, scattered the goods, and roughly treated the shopkeepers. The leading citizens did their utmost to stop the riot, promising if the people would disperse no further notice would be taken of their proceedings, but the authorities would not accept these conditions, and attempted to punish the ringleaders. This action gave rise to more rioting, but the Government ultimately dropped the matter, fearing that the rioting might be taken up in London.

Attempts were made to stop all decorations,

and if anyone had the hardihood to disobey the mandates of the Christmas-haters, considerable trouble ensued. Sometimes, however, the zeal of the authorities brought them into ridicule. A rather amusing instance may be cited. A man in the Metropolis put up a quantity of Christmas greenery, and the Lord Mayor hearing of it, instructed one of his men to go and take it down. The poor fellow met with a warm reception from the London 'prentice boys, and had to make a hasty retreat without fulfilling his mission. The great civic dignitary, mounted on horseback, next appeared on the scene, presuming, no doubt, that his coming would suffice to quell the unruly mob; but it was not so his Lordship was received with jeers and laughter. The noise frightened his horse, and it rushed off at full speed, to the delight of the assembly.

In place of the merry chimes which formerly welcomed Christmas from every church steeple in the land, the crier passed along the silent streets of the towns, ringing his harsh-sounding bell, and proclaiming in a monotonous voice: " No Christmas! No Christmas!"

Preaching in churches was proscribed, but there were always some ready to set at defiance

the laws of the new Parliament. The country
gentlemen in not a few cases guarded the doors
of the churches during the time the forbidden
services were being conducted. • This was so
even in the very shadow of the building where
the Commons met and made their laws against
the celebration of Christmas. We learn that at
St. Margaret's, Westminster, not only was a
sermon preached, but the church was decorated
with evergreens. The churchwarden and clerk
had to appear before the Committee entrusted
with trying and punishing those who broke the
laws relating to this season. " The churchwarden," we find it recorded, " excused himself
on the ground that he opened the church at
the request of the parishioners, who, having met
to consider how they should spend their Christmas,
had come to the conclusion that as so few would
work, and none open shop, on Christmas Day,
they might draw people into church to hear a
sermon who would else misspend their time in
taverns ; as to the greenery, for that the sexton
was responsible." The next question asked was
rather more serious—Why the preacher selected
was one who had made himself prominent against
Parliament ? Mr. Churchwarden, in reply, said

that "The clergyman in question had not long before preached at Chelsea, before some of the members, and if he were permitted to preach at Chelsea, he could not see why he might not do the same at Westminster." His arguments were received in a favourable light, and he escaped with an admonition. We learn that another clergyman was served with a warrant during the delivery of his sermon, and the next day was taken into custody.

The Reformers in Scotland were active in trying to stop the observance of Christmas, and were more successful than the authorities in England. The Kirk-Session Books of Scotland include many notes bearing on this subject, and the Rev. W. W. Tulloch, D.D., has unearthed and reproduced a few of the more curious entries. " In St. Andrews, in 1573," says Mr. Tulloch, "several persons had to make open satisfaction for observing Yule-day." On the 21st December, 1649, the Kirk-Session of the ancient city decreed that intimation be made from the pulpit "that no Yule be keepit, but that all be put to work as ane ordinar work day, with certification that those who are any idlers shall be taken notice of and be severlie censured."

In conformity with this judgment, a month later
several persons were charged with playing jollie
at the goose on Yule day, and were condemned
for the next two Sabbaths "to be in the old
College Kirk, and to be examined, and to sit
altogether upon ane form, before the publick
congregation, and to be rebuked for their fault."
In 1683, the bakers of Glasgow were warned
to discontinue the practice of baking Yule bread.
To show their utter contempt for the day, the
Reformers enjoined that the wives and servants
were to spin in open sight of the people upon
Yule day, and that the farm labourers were to
yoke their ploughs. One John Wylie, in the
year 1605, escaped the censure of the Kirk-
Session of Dundonald for "nott yoking his
plough on Yuil day" by declaring that it was
undergoing repairs at "the smiddie."

Masques, which had been so popular in the
mansions of the nobility, were forbidden, and the
theatres were closed. History shows that for a
long period the poor player was held in low
esteem. All players, in the days of Queen
Elizabeth, unless acting as servants to some earl
or baron, were liable to imprisonment, and the
aristocracy had thus a monopoly of stage perform-

ances. According to the history of Hull, in the year 1598 the Mayor of Hull issued an order denouncing " divers idle lewd persons, players, or setters out of plays, tragedies, comedies, and interludes," who frequented the town ; and it is further stated that every man or woman who should be found at the acting of any of the plays "should forfeit 2s. 6d. for every time and offence." In Puritan England, not only were spectators fined, but actors were whipped at the cart's tail. Dancing on the rope, puppet shows, games at bowls, and horse racing were regarded with displeasure. Bear-baiting, a popular pastime with high and low, was stopped.

Earnest attempts were made to improve the morals of the people, but the zeal of the Puritans was often not tempered with mercy, and frequently displayed a want of common-sense. It was enacted that adultery should be punished with death, and many other laws were equally severe.

The epoch of the Commonwealth ended with the death of Cromwell, and the house of Stuart was restored, Charles II. being called to the throne of his ancestors. Christmas once more became a popular holiday, and merriment again prevailed in old England.

Under the Mistletoe Bough.

"Holly berries! holly berries! gleaming through the prickly
    screen,
Heralds of old Father Christmas, with his wreaths of ever-
    green;
Keeping warm our hearts within us in the time of falling
    snow,
You are bright, but much brighter is a sprig of mistletoe."

                              —Horace Lennard.

T HE historical associations of the mistletoe
carry us back to an early period in the
annals of our country. It has formed a pleasing
theme for the pen of the poet, with the maiden it
has often been the commencement of a bright
future, and it brings gladness to the stately hall
and humble cottage, cheering alike the rich and
the poor.

In the hanging up of the mistletoe bough we
have a relic of the worship of our pagan ancestors.
Let us carry back our thoughts to the days of the
ancient Britons, and to the time of their winter-
solstice. A solemn procession is formed, with the
Druid priests at the head. They make their way
to the forest, until the most stately of the oaks is

reached, where a grass altar is raised, and on the trunk of the tree are inscribed the names of the most powerful amongst their deities. Two white bulls are fastened to the oak, and next the Arch-Druid, clad in white robes (the emblem of purity), ascends the tree. He carries in his hand a con-secrated golden pruning-hook, and crops the mistletoe, and under the tree stand priests holding a fine white cloth or the folds of their garments, ready to catch it as it falls. If by accident any reaches the ground, it is regarded as an evil omen, and they believe that some dire misfortune will occur. Next the bulls, and sometimes even human beings, are sacrificed, and festivities follow. The mistletoe is divided into small pieces, and distributed amongst the bystanders, who with great care carry it to their homes and place it over their doors as a propitiation and shelter to the sylvan deities during the season of frost and snow. The ceremony is performed when the moon is six days old. These singular rites, it is recorded, lingered in the country after the Romans held the power in the land, and for a considerable time under the Jutes, Saxons, and Angles.

Odin's second son, Balder, the god of poetry and eloquence, dreamt that his death was

imminent, and in the travail of his spirit con-
fided the ominous news to Friga, his mother.
She, with all a mother's anxiety, laid an injunction
on the forces of nature—on the elements, on wild
beasts, and noxious plants—that they should work
no evil upon her son, and bound them by oath to
her will. Then, when the gods closed in battle,
Balder took his place amid the communion of
swords and the hail of arrows. But Balder's
enemy, Loki, saw that the hero was invulnerable
to the weapons of the combatants, and craftily
disguised himself as an aged woman, and sought
Friga, to whom he extolled Balder for his valour
and happy fortune; whereon the goddess explained that the forces of nature were bound by
oath to abstain from any evil action against the
hero, the mistletoe alone being exempt from the
obligation, as it was too feeble and insignificant to
work mischief. Then Loki eagerly gathered
the fatal parasite, and hastened to the assembly of
the gods. Heda, the blind, became the agent of his
evil design. Being asked why he did not contend
with Balder and his shafts, he replied that he was
blind and unarmed; whereon Loki furnished
him with an arrow of mistletoe, and directed him
to shoot, Balder being before him. Then Heda

drew his bow, and launched the fatal arrow against his victim. True to its mission, it smote and slew the unfortunate son of Odin.

Shakespeare refers to the mistletoe in *Titus Andronicus*, ii. 3; and Tamora, Queen of the Goths, speaks of it as the *baneful mistletoe*. She says :—

> " Have I not reason, think you, to look pale?
> These two have 'ticed me hither to this place,
> A barren, detested vale you see it is ;
> The trees, though summer, yet forlorn and lean,
> O'ercome with moss, and baneful mistletoe."

The poet Gay speaks of introducing the mistletoe into the decorations of churches at Christmastide. He writes :—

> " When rosemary and bays, the poet's crown,
> Are bawl'd in frequent cries through all the town ;
> Then judge the festival of Christmas near,
> Christmas, the joyous period of the year !
> Now with bright holly all the temples strow,
> With laurel green, and sacred *mistletoe*."

Dr. William Stukeley, in his " Medallic History of Carausius," published 1757-59, adverts to the old practice of bringing mistletoe into York Minster. Stukeley says : " This was the most respectable festival of our Druids, called Yule-tide ; when mistletoe, which they called *all-heal*, was carried in their hands, and laid on their altars, as an

emblem of the salutiferous advent of Messiah.
This mistletoe they cut off the trees with their
upright hatchets of brass, called celts, put upon
the ends of their staffs, which they carried in
their hands. Innumerable are these instruments
found all over the British Isles. The custom is
still preserved in the north, and was lately
observed at York ; on the eve of the Christmas
Day they carry mistletoe to the high altar of the
cathedral, and proclaim a public and universal
liberty, pardon, and freedom to all sorts of inferior
and even wicked people at the gates of the city,
towards the four quarters of the heaven." We
need not remind our readers that the mistletoe is
banished from the church decorations, we presume
on account of its Druidical associations. John
Brand, M.A., thinks that Gay was in error in
speaking of the mistletoe as forming part of the
Christmas church decoration. He made inquiries
at many churches, but could not discover it being
used. In the olden time mistletoe was believed
to be a powerful charm against witchcraft; to-day
it has a fascination over witches of a more charming character.

It is generally understood that each white berry
on the mistletoe bough denotes or represents a

kiss, and should be plucked from the bough when the pleasing ceremony has been performed, so that the stripping of the berries denotes the extent to which the kissing has been carried. Mr. Wilton Jones writes on this agreeable theme :- -

> " Many a manly heart is light,
>   Many a rose-decked bosom heaves
> Under the gleam of the berries white,
>   Set in the clusters of spear-shaped leaves.
> What is the use of the mistletoe now?
>   What can its purpose be? Only this -
> Honour the ancient Druidical bough,
>   It gives such a charming excuse for a kiss."

The middle of the seventeenth century is the earliest period in which allusion is found to kissing under the mistletoe.

Here we may introduce a few notes concerning kissing. In Biblical and classic times we find it a common mode of salutation. Job declares he was free from the superstition of kissing the hand to the heavenly bodies. The hand was likewise kissed to Baal. The lips, hands, or feet were variously kissed by the Greeks ; while the Romans, from the familiar salutation of the lips, settled into the custom of respectfully kissing the hands of their great men. The people of Carthage,

too, had distinct kissing customs, the right hands
being kissed simultaneously, and then the lips.
Thus, from one ancient source or another, the
pleasure-fraught observances of the subject have
come down to us.

In the works of Shakespeare are many references to the kissing customs of his day.
Much time was spent at taverns, and it was
usual to courteously salute the hostess, a custom
alluded to in the *Merry Wives of Windsor.*
Hence it was that the popularity of an inn
depended in a measure upon the attractions of
the hostess or her daughters.

The act of kissing was a chief element in
betrothals, being, as it were, a seal to the contract.
In *Twelfth Night* (Act v., S. 1,) we find this
noted ; the priest says :

> "A contract of eternal bond of love,
>   Confirmed by mutual joinder of your hands,
>   Attested by the holy close of lips,
>   Strengthened by interchangement of your rings ;
>   And all the ceremony of this compact,
>   Sealed in my function, by my testimony,"

while we may judge, partly from old missals, but
chiefly from allusions and descriptions, that kissing
was as much a part of the ceremonial of marriage
as of betrothal.   How the retiring decorum a

bride might prefer is rudely dispelled by
Petruchio, in the *Taming of the Shrew*, when he

> "Took the bride about the neck
> And kissed her lips with such a clamorous smack
> That at the parting all the church did echo."

This connection of kissing as part of a bond
has further allusion in *King John*. Philip says :—

> "Young princes, close your hands,"

and the Duke of Austria rejoins :—

> "And your lips, too ; for I am well assured
> That I did so when I was first assured."

So again in *King Richard II.*, the king, on
being informed that he is to be separated from
his wife in banishment, bursts into the following
touching exclamation :—

> "Doubly divorced ! Bad men, you violate
> A two-fold marriage, 'twixt my crown and me,
> And then betwixt me and my married wife.
> Let me unkiss the oath 'twixt thee and me ;
> And yet not so, for with a kiss 'twas made."

In many parts of England the kissing bough is
constructed of holly, and it is of "The Kiss
Beneath the Holly" that Mrs. Hobson Farrand
writes the following lines :—

> "'Be merry and wise,' says the good old song,
> And joy to the heart that penned it,
> If we've ought to fret, the stately 'pet'
> Will never reform or mend it.

" On Christmas night, when the log burns bright,
   To be joyous is not folly ;
There's nought amiss in the playful kiss
   That's stolen beneath the holly.

" Let hand clasp hand with a hearty clasp,
   To all give a welcome greeting ;
Fling pride afar ; don't gloom or mar
   The coming Christmas meeting.
' Be merry and wise,' say sparkling eyes,
   Away with all melancholy—
There's nought amiss, just laugh at the kiss
   That's stolen beneath the holly.

" Oh, welcome with glee the festive night,
   When the joyous bells are ringing ;
But once a year the chime we hear,
   That the Christmas time is bringing.
Don't pout or frown 'neath the mystic crown —
   To be joyous is not folly ;
There's nought amiss in the Christmas kiss
   That's stolen beneath the holly."

Index.

www.ingramcontent.com/pod-product-compliance
Lightning Source LLC
Chambersburg PA
CBHW020350030726
47496CB00007B/2085